SMALL
BUSINESS IN
TOUGH
TIMES

SMALL BUSINESS IN **TOUGH** TIMES

John Day

LOTHIAN BOOKS

ACKNOWLEDGEMENTS

The author would like to thank the following people: Robert Gottliebsen, for his positive foreword; David Crawford, chartered accountant, for his general business advice; Tim Wildash, marketer, for his enthusiasm and ideas; Ian Gilbert, lawyer, for his contribution on insolvency administrations; Graham Levie, lawyer, for his suggestions on dealing with financial troubles; Kevin Burt, bank manager, Sue Day, chartered accountant, Ross Dobinson, company director, and Jim Smith, chartered accountant, for checking the complete text; and Sylvia Bradshaw for her inspiration.

A Lothian book

Lothian Publishing Company Pty Ltd
A division of Thomas C. Lothian Pty Ltd
11 Munro Street, Port Melbourne, Victoria 3207

National Library of Australia
Cataloguing-in-publication data:

Day, John.
    Small business in tough times.

    ISBN 0 85091 454 X.

    1. Small business — Management. I. Title.

658.022

Edited by White Kite Productions
Cover design by Robin Cowpe
Text designed by Robin Cowpe

Typeset in Century Old Style by Bookset, Melbourne
Printed by Impact Printing (Vic.) Pty Ltd, Melbourne

Royalties from the sale of this book are
being donated to the Paidion Foundation.

Foreword

When *Business Review Weekly* started publication in 1981 we decided to write a profile of a small- or medium-sized enterprise each week. At the time people told us we couldn't do it, that there would never be enough subjects. That was ten years ago and over that period we have described the operations and motivations of more than five hundred enterprises in our 'Up and Comers' column and in other parts of the magazine.

Australia has a wonderful spirit of enterprise or, as John Day might say, 'we have a great many enterprisers'. Not all 'Up and Comers' will make it through 1991. Indeed, in the past year or so, there has been a higher than usual casualty rate amongst small businesses. It is important to understand why this has happened and to examine how it is affecting the nation. When you study John Day's book you will see that he places a great deal of emphasis on the preparation of the business plan, and on monitoring the money that is coming in, and that is likely to come in, to an enterprise, and the amount that is likely to go out.

Recessions always take a toll of small and large businesses that are highly borrowed, because their forecasts are overly optimistic. This time around there has been an additional element. Many of our 'Up and Comers' casualties effectively mortgaged their profits by borrowing money to invest in the property market, using negative gearing to reduce tax payments. Had they worked to a carefully prepared plan to concentrate their capital and effort on the business they had chosen, more might have survived the crunch and now be in a position to prosper. Banks that lent money to these businesses in the belief that property would hold its value have been taken to the cleaners with these businesses. As a result, at the beginning of 1991, banks had many of their best executives collecting debts and managing problem accounts.

The experiences of the past twelve to eighteen months will dissuade many people from starting their own businesses, and make bankers very nervous. This will be unfortunate for the 'enterprisers', for banks, and for the nation as a whole. But that time will no doubt pass and commonsense will prevail — particularly as many former executives of large corporations are looking to establish a new life now that the big companies are no longer offering job security.

Always remember that banks receive small margins when dealing with large corporations. The most profitable business for banks, outside the housing market, is sound loans to smaller enterprises, and so the position for small businesses will surely improve. During the coming decade ways to provide equity capital for the better small enterprises will increase. Smaller enterprises are major employers of labour because they usually can use it far more efficiently than large corporations that require layers of management.

The coming years will see opportunities for smaller enterprises increase generally. Not only will more government work be contracted out to more efficient smaller groups, but larger corporations will turn to smaller enterprises to undertake certain functions. (The giant McDonald's corporation franchises out its stores rather than operate them itself, and one of the secrets of the Japanese success in the motor vehicle industry is the large network of smaller component manufacturers that are aided by communal computer and other developmental facilities.) So don't despair if life is tough at the moment; the future is on your side if your business or your plan is good.

As you face this time of optimism, I commend John Day's book to you.

Robert Gottliebsen
Chairman and Editorial Director,
BRW Publications

Contents

Preface

The changing connotation of the word *entrepreneur* testifies to the power of the media as image makers. It also highlights the responsibility faced by anyone who runs or participates in a business; and, directly or indirectly, that includes a great many of us.

Originally, the word *entrepreneur* simply meant someone who undertakes business activities with the prospect of making a loss or a profit. It was associated with risk-taking, courage, daring — traits regarded as typically Australian. It also involved notions of having (and giving others) a fair go, and of being unafraid to make a sacrifice in order to reap long-term rewards.

Recently, though, the tone has soured. Some entrepreneurs have developed a reputation as exploiters, callous parasites who ignore the consequences of their greed. Their flamboyant schemes to 'get rich quick' have all but eclipsed the humble endeavours of mere workers, the irony being that many a tycoon was once such a worker.

In order to shed these connotations we must look for a new word to describe the person who goes into business to make something out of nothing, to take on and win the challenge of financial independence in a materialistic society. In this book I have replaced the word *entrepreneur* with the slightly old-fashioned word *enterpriser*. I hope this may help to recapture the spirit of small business in Australia.

Thanks again to the media's quest for 'scoops' and 'beat-ups', much of the business news that reaches the wider population is not only negative but also pertains to BIG business only. Except in the better quality financial press, the small business story has for too long been overlooked in the rush for sensational coverage.

Stories about small business are invariably stories about people like you and me, stories about both success and failure. As such they are always interesting and I have included some of them here, trusting that they will inform, challenge, warn, encourage, reassure or inspire readers.

There are three phases in a business career: getting there, being there, and staying there. In particularly tough times, a fourth phase is introduced: getting out. The four parts of this book deal with these four phases. Even if you have already made it in business and are tempted to go straight to part three, I urge you to read the first two parts as well. Like a human life, in which childhood events have a profound influence on adulthood, a business career is set in the early stages of its development. Thus, a re-examination of your past business activities might throw light on your present and your future prospects. Unlike a human life, though, a business career can have any number of comebacks; and some of the comments, advice and anecdotes offered in parts one and two might prompt you to do things differently in your next business, should you find yourself starting all over again.

JKD

Introduction

It is not easy to define small business. A small business can be a one-person band or a concern employing a hundred people. In the USA a business is deemed 'small' if it is independently owned and operated and is not dominant in its field of operation. In Australia the Small Business Development Corporation and the Real Estate Act classify as 'small' any business whose value is less than $100,000, exclusive of stock and plant — that is, goodwill only. A report by the Australian Committee on Small Businesses as far back as 1971 defines as small 'a business in which one or two persons are required to make all the critical management decisions — finance, accounting, personnel, purchasing, processing or servicing, marketing and selling — without the aid of internal specialists and with specific knowledge in only one or two functional areas'. For the purposes of this book, a business is considered 'small' if it is not big enough to employ its own financial expert.

Operating a small business in tough times should be the same as operating a small business in easy times: it is always a challenge and a struggle. But there is nothing like an economic recession to remind all players of the golden rules on which every commercial enterprise should be built. It is interesting that many of the enterprisers who flourish in easy times, and make a great show of their gains, are the first to go to the wall in

1

tough times, while many middle-of-the road, low-profile operators manage to pull through, with hardly a waver in their profits.
The reason for this is simply that the basic principles of
successful business are perennial — they never change.

In some ways the crisis point brought about by adverse
conditions beyond their control is a blessing in disguise for small
business operators, because it forces them to appreciate first-
hand the grounds on which these principles are built. Lessons
learnt through personal failure always hit harder than abstract
ones. And where there is pain there is an incentive to avoid a
repetition of the experience that caused that pain. ('No gain
without pain', as the saying goes.) This book will therefore be of
value to all people who operate, or want to operate, a small
business — in tough times, in all times.

Apart from the perennial issues that underlie business success, there are some measures that can be used to cope in
emergencies. These serve as first-aid only and should not take
precedence over longer term priorities. They might involve
changing the schedule and sequence of planned business activities, or perhaps a shift of emphasis from one area to another, or
the suspension or delay of development plans. Whatever means
is chosen to overcome an immediate crisis, it should be remembered that the economy moves in cycles. Sooner or later, tough
times will lighten up into easier times; and once the good times
have returned they will eventually fade into bad again. Basically,
the two sets of conditions are at opposite ends of a spectrum,
and the pendulum of economic cycles swings between them.
Because the one extreme causes the other, each can be used to
prepare for the other.

Ups and downs in the economy might also be seen as
mountains and valleys: rather than stare gloomily into the
abyss, small business operators should fix one eye on the other
side and brace themselves for the crossing. By treating all
problems as a learning experience, small business operators can
reinvest their enhanced knowledge in their own future, thereby
turning a negative situation to their ultimate advantage. In tough
times the immediate priority is to survive — survive this crisis
in order to prosper in the future.

PART ONE: GETTING THERE

CHAPTER 1

The Person Behind the Business

THE ENTERPRISING TYPE

It is interesting to ask self-employed people what made them leave the security of a good job to strike out on their own. Most say they did so either to escape from unemployment, actual or anticipated; to establish a source of supplementary income; or so that they could be their own boss. Some say they are basically insecure and must prove their worth on their own. Others claim that they are bored by the slow pace in a large company and hunger for more action. Others even say that they were motivated by a nagging spouse, by a desire to keep up with the Joneses, or by a hero in business (discover the identity of an enterpriser's hero and you will learn a lot about him or her).

If money ever enters the picture, it is usually in the form of the rhetorical question, 'Why should I get only fifteen per cent of the revenue I am earning when I could get a hundred per cent?' Why, indeed? Only very few self-employed people describe themselves as capitalists in the traditional sense of hoping to accumulate substantial profits. Although, by definition, the achievement of wealth must be the ultimate aim of any enterpriser, a fascination with the process of *getting there* is a more common motivating factor.

The typical enterpriser is a strong individualist and a born optimist. To him or her the bucket is not half empty but half full.

This trait is sometimes taken to excess; but surviving the false starts, near-failures and disappointments that enterprisers face every day does, indeed, require undying optimism. The word *enterprise* therefore equates with the word *optimism*. The enterpriser sees solutions, not problems, and finds an opportunity where others might find despair.

CASE STUDY:

Jim is a fellow who grew up in quite a business-like family and was destined from the start to be enterprising. He is the epitome of an enterpriser. He sleeps no more than six hours a night. In the mornings he reads every available newspaper and takes his own clippings. He files everything according to subject headings. He calls himself a public relations man. Jim is into contacts, he knows all the 'right' people — not because of his family but because he makes an effort to meet such people. He joins the 'right' clubs and develops the 'right' contacts. He is always building, looking for ideas, looking for opportunities.

At the beginning of the current economic downturn, rather than grizzle, Jim went out and borrowed four or five books about the depressions of the 1890s and the 1930s to look for opportunities to make some money. He concluded that the number of poor people was likely to increase and, given that the cheapest nutritional meal is fish, he set up a business supplying fish to the Salvation Army.

A popular misconception is that the enterpriser is willing to accept risks and to gamble. In fact, most enterprisers are not as inclined to take risks as many people would think. Rather than back the 10–1 shot, they tend to go for the 3–1 shot. Whether at leisure or in business, successful enterprisers set themselves exciting but realistic goals, which they attain or exceed.

Self-employment gives you freedom of choice. You work in the area which appeals to you and devote as many hours as you wish to *your* business, to the execution of *your* ideas. One of the main reasons people go into their own business is so that they can be justly rewarded for their efforts, skill and expertise. But the rewards may be a long time coming, therefore patience and perseverance are required.

Admittedly the self-employed face more uncertainty than people who remain in paid employment, but in hard times even the jobs of employees are not secure, along with their employers' survival.

CASE STUDY:

Brian is a very competent accountant and has been a close friend of mine for many years. Recently he relocated to a country area to work for a new company. He put his heart and soul into his job, living in a caravan for many months away from his family, and finally buying a home in the country town where he worked. The very day his family was shifting, his wife was killed in a car accident. Less than six months later the business was sold and Brian, then aged 55, was retrenched. Where could he go?

The uncertainty of self-employment simply means that you need to have a strong ego, that you cannot afford to be easily discouraged, that you must plough on without stopping to justify yourself. To try and to fail is better than not to try at all.

To prosper in your own business you must be honest, especially with yourself, and be able to enjoy your undertaking, make the most of it, make it work *for* you, not *against* you. Above all, you must have plenty of self-discipline — discipline to adhere to your plans, honour your commitments, work the required hours and produce a quality product on time and at the quoted price. You must take pride in your efforts. In small business, just as in sport, a true champion is never satisfied and develops the killer instinct to continue to strive, to achieve greater goals.

Setting up and running your own business, and managing to survive, is the ultimate test of whether you are the enterprising type. You make the decisions and you are responsible only to yourself. If the business succeeds, the resulting pride and satisfaction are yours alone; and if it fails only you can be blamed.

CASE STUDY:

Paul wanted to set up a retail clothing business. For many years he had worked for well-known companies, such as Myer and others. He had progressed from buying to marketing to retail sales and did a small stint in account collections and term layby sales. In other words, he had a fairly well-grounded career, but at the age of twenty-six he had little money and no experience in running a small business. What he did have were apparently innate enterprising characteristics. He embarked on a number of courses, read lots of books and did some feasibility studies. From his experience with the larger chains, he knew all about mark-ups, and was in touch with the relevant suppliers and buyers of clothing. He set about doing his business plan.

Paul needed much less sleep than the average person. In the first twelve months of setting up his business he was constantly making notes. When questioned about this he said, 'While my mind's working, while I am being productive, I can concentrate. As things come to mind I document them. I don't want to take the subordinate or the lazy attitude of the nine-to-fiver. I am going to concentrate on making this business successful.'

Three years later Paul's business is successful. He has opened up two extra menswear shops under his own label. He enjoys good profits and now has a little more time to himself; and when required he still rolls up his sleeves.

BORN TO DO BUSINESS?

One often hears it said that someone was 'born to be in business'. It is certainly true that to be successful in business you have to be able to cope with stress, frustration, disappointment and other intellectual rigours as well as physical ones. Any hereditary factor or childhood conditioning which fosters such traits will therefore assist in coping.

Statistics tell us that the archetypal successful enterpriser in Australia tends to have had relevant, rather than lengthy, education, had demanding but encouraging parents, seeks high levels of achievement and is motivated to own and operate a business, has undertaken lots of planning, is happily married, is physically fit, tends towards aggressive (motivated by self-interest) and detached (independent and unemotional) modes of interpersonal behaviour, and has the mental and emotional capacity to handle the task.

Allowing for the inevitable over-simplification of such a model, we can readily recognise many aspects of this stereotype. Most enterprisers enjoy talking about their childhood and most of the time their recollection of their earlier years makes fascinating listening. They were interesting and unusual children, carrying out duties around the house or delivering newspapers to earn money for a new bike, and starting up collections of stamps, coins, rocks, and so on. Underlying these activities, which were ostensibly a source of fun, was always the prospect of gain and growth.

The mature enterpriser's obsessive need to achieve may often be traced to his or her childhood relationship with the more dominant parent. Even if Mum or Dad was not a great commercial success, admiration and a desire for approval drove the child to prove him- or herself. Subtle signs of recognition from the parent, such as a nod or a smile, were cherished rewards. A surprisingly large number of enterprisers are the offspring of self-employed parents whose free spirit and independence rubbed off. In cases where the parent/child relationship was less cordial, even strained, the grown-up child may be out to get the 'oldie' by achieving a greater level of success in order to prove superiority. Finally, if there was no breadwinner because of death, divorce or desertion during the enterpriser's childhood, the child may have been forced to assume this role in the family. Inheriting a great deal of responsibility at an early age can speed along maturity, and with it enterprising tendencies.

WHAT ARE YOUR MOTIVES AND QUALIFICATIONS?

The fact that you are reading this book probably means that you consider yourself the enterprising type, and you may even have decided that you were, indeed, born to do business. But what is your motive for going out on your own?

Is it that you are just a dreamer? Or is it that you are sick and tired of being told what to do and you want your so-called freedom? Is it that you feel unappreciated or undervalued, or that you want to get back at the boss? Rather than good reasons to start your own business, these are simply reasons to quit your current job.

Is it that you want to make money? As I said earlier, this must be one of your aims; but this motive alone is not enough to get you through the difficult years.

Don't go into business if you think that the grass is greener on the other side of the fence. Don't go into business if you have the attitude of a nine-to-fiver and enjoy such perks as company cars, luncheons, travel and free pens. Along with these you will also have to say goodbye to your large pension or superannuation and face up to the fact that the laws in this country tend to be in the employee's favour, not the employer's. Don't go into business just because your friends do, because your family always has, or because you can't get permanent employment.

CASE STUDY:

Sammy was only twenty-five. He had been married two or three years and had a very supportive wife. His older brother had a furniture business in which Sammy worked for wages. The brother constantly harassed Sammy and put him down. Sammy dreamed of going into business for himself, but his motive was purely to beat his bullying brother, to avenge him.

Well, he did. But he didn't do a business plan, and he didn't do anything else recommended in this book. The

---

result was that within three months he hadn't sold any furniture, he couldn't pay his rent and he had lost $15,000 — his life savings.

Fortunately he was young enough to recover his losses. And he also learnt a lesson about healthy motives.

Starting a new business is not a time for self-deception. It is more often cause for great worry and tension as you put in long hours to do the necessary groundwork. Many small business operators risk not only their house (to raise capital) but also their family life, their health and their mental well-being. Big companies can afford to make some mistakes; small ones can't.

It is important to have positive reasons for going into business. Some sound motives, especially in combination, are:

- to develop a new sense of independence and freedom;
- to develop creative ideas;
- to achieve a better lifestyle;
- to build up a personal or family asset;
- to produce a particular product or service;
- to do things better than your employer does.

Equally important is to have the necessary practical qualifications. Are you self-disciplined, motivated and creative? Are you versatile? Are you trained and experienced? Do you have knowledge of the industry you plan to go into? Do you have experience in it? Do you have the ability to motivate others? Do you have the willingness to learn? Do you have the support of your family? Do you have sufficient capital to finance the business? Do you have a strong work ethic? Do you have the ability to work under stress?

Preparation for going into business involves a critical examination of your own characteristics and capabilities. Any shortcomings should be honestly admitted and sorted out by training or guidance.

DOING YOUR HOMEWORK

You do not have to go in blind. You can get help (and relief from uncertainty) from courses, books, pamphlets, government departments, consultants (accountants, lawyers, and so on) and the experience of others. That doesn't mean you have to take every course, read everything, listen to everybody. What it does mean is that you should try to map out the terrain in which you intend to travel. Recognising the importance of planning will set you apart from the majority of people in paid employment and those who fail in self-employment. Simply to survive in today's business environment (let alone to prosper), small business people must be better informed and more professional than ever before. They must grapple with a vast array of complex issues.

Before going into business you should inform yourself about the general economy, government regulations, State, Federal and local zonings and product standard regulations, not to mention industrial relations matters, arbitration and conciliation, interest rates, exchange rates, levels of protection, levels of government and consumer spending, levels of taxation and grants, and export incentives and rebates.

Look at business in general: watch, learn, listen. Do your research, go to the libraries, use all the government resources, go to the employer associations, go to the Small Business Development Corporation. There is a huge array of books available on small business, not just on how to do business plans but on specific subjects — for example, the road transport industry, hairdressing industry, franchising, and so on. Read the newspapers and business magazines, watch the Sunday-morning business programmes on television and listen to the business shows on the radio. This way you will learn about the macro-economic environment — in other words, what is happening with oil prices, real estate prices, the world economy, the national balance of payments, the world peace programme, conservation issues. All the information that you gather from the media will eventually affect the way you run your business.

At first you may not realise how much you are learning and how it might relate to your circumstances, but eventually your knowledge will pay dividends and the relevance will become clear. If you understand what is happening in the world, you will be in a position to predict and respond to changes in interest rates, to make investment decisions and to make sales (see pages 111–114).

Finally, you should undertake thorough research into the particular industry you are contemplating entering: its sales and profit trends, the attitude of government, the effect of public opinion on profits, the level of imports, tariff protection, the economic cycles, characteristics of successful competitors, significant barriers to entry, spread of products, spread of customers, present market shares, the norm in terms of prices and products or promotions.

You should understand the requirements of your business and why a plan is so important (see chapter 3), what cash reserves you need to contribute, what you need to borrow, what levels of skills and expertise you need, what human resources you need to employ. You should assess the market and consumer needs as well as the effect of financial, legal and personal aspects of your business plan, such as the need to get a long lease to protect your tenancy. You should assess the overheads involved: wages, electricity, rent, and so on.

If you are looking at buying an existing business (see pages 20–25), find out whether goodwill has been fairly assessed. Get sound accounting and legal advice apropos of the business. What are the lease conditions, patents, trade names, business names, sources of finance, financial management systems, bookkeeping procedures, stock-buying policies, and so on? It is a good idea to insist on a two-week trial period as a condition of sale to verify claims about turnover, gross and net profit, and average weekly net figures. Sit outside the business for a few days in a row. Witness the clientele first-hand, don't just rely on an accountant's figures (which, after all, might be rubbery).

In planning any business venture begin by testing the water. Perhaps run a pilot before you commit yourself — work for someone in a similar industry, even work for the business you are thinking of buying. This enables you not only to learn about how that world operates but also to pick up valuable ideas and even clients. The hidden agenda — the culture, the clients, the suppliers and so forth — contains valuable information. But make sure you do the work yourself, don't rely on anyone else. Whatever the product or service — scrap metal, hairdressing, engineering, graphic design — do your own research, do your own homework.

Then do a careful analysis of your costs and returns. Make a realistic assessment of the competition and an honest appraisal of your own talents. Make sure you set up adequate and efficient management systems: they contribute more to business prosperity than marketing or production skills do. Make sure that you have clear objectives and be prepared to communicate these to all the people working for you and around you.

Be careful, but don't be intimidated by the things that could go wrong. Be aware when you are starting up that your competition could try to sabotage you — by painting across your windows, for example. These initial hiccups shouldn't matter; if you are determined and committed you will see them through and you will prosper.

What if you do all your research, you do your pilot study, you begin your business plan and then you decide not to go into business after all? You may decide that you are not really cut out for it just yet (and that is not to say that you won't be in the future). Fine, you are better off turning back than pressing on and causing discontentment to yourself and everyone around you. Continue to look at the alternatives. Continue to do your research, especially into the market, to find the product or service which is going to be profitable. Look at different angles, different marketing edges for ideas. Keep thinking, keep dreaming, keep looking, keep going to courses. A little down the track you might be better off, particularly in view of the hard economic environment in Australia at the moment.

DEVELOPING ENTERPRISING HABITS

Providing you do decide to go ahead, make sure that you remain one hundred per cent committed to your decision: believe in yourself and your ideas. Expect to succeed, and visualise that success by concentrating on developing certain key enterprising characteristics. These should include:

- self-discipline (the ability to establish plans and rigidly adhere to them);
- a pleasing manner, honesty, trustworthiness and reliability;
- a strong will to grow;
- freedom in decision-making and ideas;
- interest in achievement;
- little or no concern with status and the opinions of others;
- far-sightedness;
- ability and willingness to deal with people;
- ability to exercise, and desire to retain, control;
- willingness to delegate;
- willingness and ability to take risks;
- awareness of the need for profit and cashflow;
- adaptability;
- willingness to work long hours;
- willingness to find and defer to a mentor.

There is a slogan 'Work smarter, not harder.' In hard times this should be modified to 'Work smarter, work harder and work longer.' But work only six days (as in the Bible), not seven. If you don't recharge your batteries you will burn them out. Spend your day of leisure doing something you enjoy. Remember to balance the books of your personal life just as you balance your accounting books. It is important to keep things in perspective and realise that, as a human being, you have many parts to your life — your personal life, your spiritual life, your social life, your physical life and your work life — and all these parts function best when they are in harmony with each other.

I recently saw a caricature of a man, beneath which the caption read: 'He spent his health to get his wealth and now he is spending his wealth to get his health again.' You need only visit the Gold Coast to see how widely applicable this is. Don't let it happen to you.

Develop trusting relationships with your business contacts — your bank manager, your accountant and lawyer, your customers and your suppliers. When your accountant gets twenty-five phone messages after having been out of the office for an hour make sure he or she returns your call first because you are a friend; and the same goes for your bank manager and your lawyer.

Identify with your business and enjoy it. After all, it is an expression of yourself, just like a painting, a poem or a construction by a builder or an engineer. Remember, when you go into business you put yourself up there in lights, subjecting yourself to the scrutiny and criticism of the public, the Australian Securities Commission (ASC), the Taxation Office, the Department of Consumer Affairs, the Trade Practices Commission, the unions, the banks and a host of other institutions, not to mention insecure individuals around you, especially those non-achievers who want to pull you down and make you pay for breaking away from the pack.

Don't let other people's attitudes get you down. Be patient, be understanding. Understand why they think the way they do and why they say what they do, especially your beloved partner or spouse. ('Where's your share of the bills? Why are you never home? Why don't you talk to me any more? We are drifting apart. The kids need a father/mother.')

Recognise your own strengths and weaknesses, and learn to harness the former and compensate for the latter. Initially, when you start up your own business, you have to manage on whatever advice you can get from the outside. As time goes on you should be able to employ or pay for consultants to help you, or take on partners to make up for your weaknesses and give you value added, allowing you to spend most of your time doing the things you do best. If you are not sure what your weaknesses are, ask people who don't like you — they will soon tell

16

you. Then go and ask people who like you. It may be that you have too many weaknesses to go into business. It is better to find this out in the planning process.

If you are facing problems, be strong. Don't let anyone else know. When you have cashflow problems the worst thing you can do is let your customers know it. Keep to yourself. Even in tough times, always have a bright, positive attitude to life and to people. Don't *ever* complain about your business. Never criticise your customers or your competition. If you do you are putting yourself down.

Don't waste time and energy worrying about money problems. Try to look objectively at the problems, address the issues, discover what is causing them. Is it lack of sales, lack of sales at the right price, lack of quality service to your clients, inability to collect money from customers, high overheads, high interest costs? Work out what the problem is and solve it. Use that energy positively, not negatively.

On the personal front, concentrate on maintaining stable relationships with your loved ones. Business is not good if it destroys relationships, as so often happens, and it is very difficult to cope with the rigours and demands of a small business without a solid foundation at home. If you have a partner, you both need to be aware of the demands and stresses that small business causes, not just in terms of cashflow but in the form of anxiety and other mental hardship, not to mention the spoilt dinners, the forgotten birthdays, the broken dates, the insecurity of it all. Involve your partner in the business, not necessarily in the day-to-day affairs but in its commitment to success. This can only be done through concentrated communication — not necessarily every day, but perhaps once a week for an hour or so. Talk to each other so that you understand each other.

Learn to manage yourself because if you can't manage yourself you certainly won't be able to manage a business. Time management is critical if you want to do justice to all aspects of your life. However, your loved ones need not only your time but your energy as well. If you have children it is a good idea to involve them in the business, let them come to the factory or the office. Of course they will say they don't want to, and they will get bored, but they have very attentive little ears that don't miss anything. This way they will learn about business well before you or I ever did. Let them see the good and bad sides of being self-employed. Should you have to work late one night, go to work late the next day or come home early. Go to the school, go and watch your child play sport in the middle of the afternoon. Do the unusual, be part of their life. Manage your time so you can spend quality time with your family. After all, remember why you are striving: apart from the challenge of the process, it is to provide a better lifestyle for yourself and your family in the future.

You should have interests outside the business — recreational, social and cultural. Leisure activity does more than rest your executive brain cells and make you a more balanced person. It gives you an interest which can continue into your retirement. Too many people devote their lives exclusively to work and crack up completely when they 'retire' at the age of fifty or sixty. They are left with nothing to occupy their time or attention and often die of sheer boredom. No one is indispensable, as you will soon prove if your prolonged absence is forced through a nervous breakdown. So always take the holiday that is owing to you. Apart from anything else, it is a good chance to see how well you have trained your second in command.

In small business you need a huge amount of self-control, particularly in hard times. This is an important ingredient of executive efficiency. It enables you to adapt to changing conditions, to deal with emergencies and to meet unexpected challenges calmly. People who regularly indulge in moods or fits of bad temper undermine their own authority and cease to command respect from those who work for them. They lose their sense of proportion and regard the smallest setback as a crisis. They antagonise and lose the co-operation of their subordinates. A few angry words can destroy in seconds the goodwill that has perhaps taken years to build up. But well-adjusted people who exercise self-discipline earn the respect of their fellows and are at peace with themselves. They can carry responsibility without strain, keep calm in emergencies; in fact, they are sound and dependable always.

Self-employed people should have high standards. You should not ask of others what you are not prepared to do for yourself. You must be prepared to commit time and energy, make some personal sacrifices. You must be completely loyal to the business and to your subordinates. To quote from a monthly letter of the Royal Bank of Canada: 'We all have faults, but there are things we will not do. Our personal code puts them beyond consideration for us.'

Throughout your business undertakings, never lose sight of the fact that the person behind the business matters more than the business in front of the person. So by all means enjoy what you do, but keep it in perspective and look after yourself.

CHAPTER 2

Setting Up

TO ESTABLISH OR TO BUY?

Should you start a new business or buy one? It's a big decision, and should normally be decided during the development of the business plan (see chapter 3).

The *advantages* of starting a new business are:
- You will have freedom of choice in all aspects of the business.
- If you have limited capital you can start on a small scale, without having to pay for goodwill.
- You can break new ground with a new idea.

The *disadvantages* of starting your own business, as we have already seen, are:
- More time, effort and hard work are needed to start up.
- Time must be spent working up a clientele, developing lines of credit and supply and building up experienced staff.
- The future is uncertain.

The *advantages* of buying an existing business are:
- Sales to existing customers provide instant income and a known cashflow.
- Relationships with banks, suppliers, and so on, are already established.

- You can work with a vendor before and after sale to get advice and perhaps help with some secondary finance.

The *disadvantages* of buying an existing business are:
- Image and policies can be difficult to change.
- The business may have depended heavily on the people you are buying it from, on their terms, personality and contacts, and may suffer from their departure.
- It is difficult to establish the value of the business. Be aware that the person selling the business will probably want more than it is really worth.

Ultimately, the decision whether to buy or start a new business has a lot to do with what makes you feel comfortable. If you don't have years of experience in the relevant area, it may be safer to buy someone else's experience, rather than try to learn from scratch and make lots of mistakes.

However, providing you follow the advice already offered in this book — do your research, run a pilot, work for somebody else — my personal advice is to start up your own business. Although both options carry dangers and risks I think it is safer to start with a clean slate. Otherwise you don't know what sort of problems you might be buying. In hard times, although there are so many cheap businesses around, there is also a proliferation of contingent liabilities. You could walk in and take over a business, such as a printing business, and all of a sudden find that the finance company comes to repossess the press. It is what you don't know that might harm you most. You don't know whether facts and figures have been falsified, or whether economic circumstances might change the rosy picture painted for you. A new council zoning might be about to come through which will affect the location of your business or a new competitive product might be about to swamp yours or undercut it in price. Even if the existing owners know about these things, they might be loath to disclose such negative information.

If, despite the dangers, you decide to buy, a number of key issues should be carefully considered. First, if the business is so profitable, why is the existing owner selling? Don't accept his or her word. Make your own discreet enquiries to establish the reason. Park outside the building or the office and carry out a thorough survey of the business. If it is a retail business, watch at different times and on different days to assess the number of customers. Don't accept figures prepared by others, even from the vendor's accountant. Do your own research.

How long has the business been on the market? A seasonal business should be bought only with careful timing. All other things being equal, it would be unwise, for instance, to miss a Christmas boom or go into an ice-cream business in autumn, especially if there are no cash reserves for the business to fall back on.

If the business is a limited company and you are acquiring the shares, legal advice should be sought about the liabilities you are assuming. The vendor's indemnities may be useless if they are not supported by assets. Check to see whether you will be eligible/liable for any current debtors/creditors or for any other payments due.

Goodwill is almost impossible to define, but basically it is the hope, and no more, that existing customers will continue to support the business under new ownership. You will probably have to pay for this asset, which depends heavily on past profits, locality, competition in the area and the previous owner's personality. Your accountant and bank manager should be able to guide you on this point.

If the business will be relying on a local trade make sure you have a good knowledge of the area. Walk around and glean the feeling of the locality. Is it declining or growing? What developments are taking place or being planned? Visit local authorities and other businesses to get answers to these questions.

At least the last three years' audited financial statements are essential to provide some indication of turnover and profit. Go through the figures with your accountant and bank manager and adjust them if necessary.

Talk to the suppliers and see whether they will stay with you. Look carefully at all the overheads and costs. Try to determine what costs will change if you take over, whether they will increase or decrease and whether there will be different kinds of costs.

Make sure the leases are long enough, not only for you to stay there but for you to fulfil whatever your business plan suggests and for you to sell the concern with five or six years still to run.

If staff are employed how well trained or qualified are they? Will they stay on? Specialised personnel in particular should be retained if at all possible.

To summarise, your evaluation of whether to buy the business should include:

- looking at why the current owner is selling (is it through ill-health or retirement, or is there something he or she knows that you don't — a highway construction or some other reason for expected loss of business?);
- careful assessment of what you are buying and how much you are spending, whether you are borrowing or using your own capital and whether you are going to get a return on that; in particular, if you are borrowing money, whether you are going to get enough profit to cover all costs, including interest on the loan;
- careful examination of a detailed breakdown of all sales, expenses and profit, both past and projected. This needs to be audited and checked independently. It won't contain warning bells because unfortunately there are not many totally genuine, honest vendors.

Buying a business without checking these things is like buying a house without making a thorough internal inspection. Free advice on the process can be obtained from a number of sources: the bank, trade associations, employer groups, neighbouring businesses, suppliers to the business, the local milk bar, local truck drivers. They can all be indirect sources of information about whether you should buy the business or not.

The next thing you should do is look at the assets. Do this in detail. Stock should be readily saleable and not stale or obsolete. Equipment needs to be reasonably modern and in working order. Replacement costs may put a burden on the business sooner than expected. Calculate conservatively what the stock is worth, whether the price is accurate, what competition it has, its quality, style, condition, balance and suitability. Is there too much stock or not enough stock being carried? Also, what furniture, fittings and equipment are included in the sale? How old are they, do they need replacing, are they in good repair, will they fall apart, what maintenance agreements are on them? Also, how collectible are the debtors and who will collect them (are they part of the purchase)?

Get customer lists, business and client records and any other assets that are available, such as trademarks. Are there many customers with a personal attachment to the seller? If you are going to lose customers because of this the purchase price should be reduced accordingly.

You should also look at the liabilities, both obvious and contingent. This area takes a lot of work. What monies are owing to creditors, when are they payable, and who is responsible for paying them? Which taxes haven't been paid (especially group tax)? What liens are there? What mortgages exist against the assets of the business? Just to get a letter of indemnity from the vendor isn't good enough, particularly if there is any doubt as to his or her financial strength. Don't rely on the vendor's statement. It often overstates turnover, takings and expenses. Particularly beware of any financial statements that are not signed by an accountant. (Accountants can be sued for signing off on any information that is incorrect.)

Whenever buying a business you should always engage the services of a solicitor as well as your accountant to make sure nothing is missed, that all the 'i's are dotted and the 't's crossed. Make sure your purchase will genuinely give you a return on your investment and help you achieve the objectives stated in your business plan. Have an agreement written into the contract of sale that you will be permitted to work in the business with the current proprietor for four weeks prior to settlement and that the vendor agrees to continue working with you for a changeover period of four weeks after settlement. This should alert you to any possible misrepresentations or problems and ensure a smooth transition of ownership.

It is important to cover, and get in writing, a number of essential points, including a list of all the assets and liabilities purchased and a statement that actual ownership does transfer vis-a-vis title details, vehicle registration and so forth. It must be clearly set out who is taking responsibility for what liabilities.

If the business you are buying is a partnership you should get a copy of the Partnership Agreement. If there is no written agreement you should find out who the partners are and whether they have authority to sell the business with assets. It may be advisable to obtain a covenant from the seller to ensure that he or she will not compete with the buyer in the same line of business for a specified period of time within a certain radius of the buyer. Such a covenant would need to be cleared with the Trade Practices Commission, of which there is a branch in each capital city.

If the business you are buying is a company you should get a certified copy of the resolution of the shareholders' meeting on the sale of the assets. In addition, to see that all is in order, you should obtain copies of the Memorandum and Articles of Association, Share Transfer books, Register of Charges and minutes of shareholders' and directors' meetings. Consider deferring payment to the vendor so that you have a better comeback in the event of misrepresentation, default in the vendor's promise not to compete, or a contingent liability.

The most difficult factor in buying a business is arriving at the price, goodwill usually being the stumbling block. But it is not the purpose of this book to discuss how to calculate selling prices or buying prices. Most general references on small business cover this topic specifically.

A business opportunity which is growing in popularity, particularly overseas, is the franchise. This industry has been booming for the last twenty years. The essence of franchising is that one party, the franchisor, who has a product, process, trade name, service or system, enters into an agreement with another party, the franchisee, whereby the franchisee is authorised to sell the product or the process, and so on. (Such agreements are also known as dealership licences and distributorships.) The franchisor in return is paid by the franchisee. The size and the form of the payment can vary according to the type of business and whether the franchisor is new or well established. The franchisor will normally look after advertising and training, and provide merchandise and advice. Because of these support systems, many small businesses start by buying a franchise. Although such arrangements rarely generate a fortune, your money can buy you good experience. However, caution should be exercised. There are some major traps in buying a franchise, not the least of which is how financially strong the franchisor is her/himself. Before taking on such a partner (and this is how you must see the franchisor: as your business partner) obtain bank references for the franchise or seek advice from the Franchise Advisory Council.

The *advantages* of a franchise are:

- It gives the small business operator an opportunity to participate in a much larger business, enabling his or her capital contribution to go further and the cost of entering at that level of business to be lower.
- The business is usually supported by marketing arrangements.
- If management systems and training are in place and enhance efficiency, the risk of failure is theoretically reduced.
- Profitability in a franchise business is, theoretically, generally higher. This allows the franchisor to expand the business more quickly at a lower capital cost and provides for better control. Because of the financial commitment and personal qualities of the franchisee as business owner and employee, he or she is more likely to contribute towards higher profit.

However, the *disadvantages* of a franchise are:

- There is a risk that the franchisor might collapse as the result of inexperience or financial instability.
- The well-conducted franchise will be closely controlled. This means that the franchisee will lose some independence, and this may cause disillusionment.
- The business may turn out to be a fad.
- The franchise arrangement might be a vehicle for fraud.
- The franchisor might have drawn up the agreement to ensure that it protects his or her interests only.

The purchase of a franchise should be contemplated in exactly the same way as any small business purchase and with just as much care, if not more.

SMALL BUSINESS STRUCTURES

If you elect to set up your own business, one of the earliest decisions you will face is how to structure it. Four options are available and careful thought should be given to the appropriateness of each of them. Your accountant should assist you in making your choice, which should be governed by the nature of the business, its estimated profitability and the degree of financial risk.

1 Sole Proprietorships

If you want to run a business by yourself, the simplest and cheapest structure to adopt is that of sole proprietor or sole operator. This can be done with the minimum of legal formalities and requirements. Individuals may wish to operate under their own name, or any other business name that has not previously been used may be chosen and registered with the ASC Business Centre in the relevant State.

The *advantages* of this type of structure are:

- A sole proprietor benefits directly from all profits and holds and owns legal title to all the business assets, both tangible and intangible, to equipment and to any goodwill. Any losses incurred by the business can be used to reduce income from other sources.

- It is easy to wind up and shut down, and reporting requirements and government regulations are simpler than for other forms of business.

The *disadvantages* are:

- Management expertise may be limited, being restricted to the competence and skill of the individual owner unless there are other salaried staff.
- Additional capital may be limited by its dependence on the personal credit rating of the sole proprietor.
- The owner has unlimited personal liability.
- The business is viable only while the owner does not suffer accident, disability or death. Insurance must be taken out to provide for these risks.
- All business profits are taxed at personal rates, which may be higher than other marginal tax rates.
- Provisional tax is payable by the self-employed person on a quarterly basis, which can be crippling in the early stages of the business.
- The owner is often forced to make all the decisions without the opportunity to test out the ideas of others.
- In the eyes of the law you and the business are one. If things go wrong you cannot, for instance, blame anyone else in the business. If bankruptcy occurs all your assets will go into a pool to pay creditors.

The continued prosperity of a sole proprietorship depends to an enormous extent upon the continuing credit, discipline, skill, knowledge, ability, judgement, experience, personality, relationships and quality of life of the sole proprietor.

To summarise, therefore, the major advantage of a sole proprietorship is the ease of setting up and administration. Despite the major disadvantage of unlimited liability, I always advise people starting off a new business to do so as a sole operator and to revise their situation regularly.

2 Partnerships

The next most common form of business structure is the partnership, including those formed by husbands and wives for taxation-splitting purposes. A business partnership is simply a relationship that exists between two or more people or entities who come together in order to carry on an enterprise with a view to making a profit.

The business name of the partnership should always be registered because it is not appropriate for any one of the parties to use his or her own name. Acts exist in all States and Territories of Australia to govern the formation and running of partnerships but they vary slightly. Under the provisions of the Companies Code throughout Australia the maximum number of people who may comprise a partnership is limited to twenty, except in the case of certain professional partnerships.

If you are considering this structure you should first ask yourself why, in fact, you want to take on a partner. Don't do it for the wrong reasons — for example, financial advantage or because you need a 'holiday'. A business partner should contribute value to the business other than just money; he or she should contribute skills which are additional or complementary to yours. Partnerships, like marriages, can be fantastic if they work out, but if they fail — if one partner becomes a liability rather than an asset — they can become a real problem and can cause quite severe financial damage.

Obviously in those situations in which the strengths and weaknesses of each partner are well balanced the business will benefit, but if the balance is tipped the partnership itself will become the business's worst enemy. It is probably no accident that some of the greatest enterprising successes have been solo acts.

Apart from greed, one of the most common reasons for the failure of both marriages and businesses is that people don't communicate with each other. They don't meet, they are not honest with each other, they don't face the real issues and the problems. That is why all business partners should be prepared to have lots of meetings, mostly formalised, and to make a real effort.

29

The *advantages* of a partnership are:

- The administrative procedures associated with establishing a new business partnership are relatively simple and inexpensive. Once a business name has been registered, the operation is simple to understand and run.
- This type of structure can enhance performance due to the complementary skills of the respective partners, and allows their strengths and weaknesses to offset each other. It also enables individuals to achieve more than they might on their own, the whole often being greater than the sum of its parts.
- There's little legal interference from government bodies.
- It is more likely that additional capital can be raised where there is more than one person involved.
- The business is less vulnerable to any one individual's disability through sickness, accident or death.

The *disadvantages,* however, are:

- Each partner still has unlimited personal liability and is responsible for the activities of the other partner(s). Unlimited personal liability attaches to the partners for any and all debts of the business partnership and this can jeopardise the personal estate of either partner.
- Partners are mutually bound and obligated and are personally responsible for each other's professional actions.
- It is difficult to change partners, particularly when disputes arise. This can cause a great deal of personal anxiety and financial loss.
- Where the partners' contributions each have a negative (rather than a positive) value, the principle that the whole can be greater than the sum of its parts works devastatingly in reverse. It is difficult to calculate the values of respective contributions for the purposes of dissolving the partnership.

- The fact that the partnership may not contain more than twenty people can limit the raising of business capital, whereas companies may raise capital through a large number of shareholders.
- The business profits are taxed at personal rates, which at the moment are higher than company rates. Partnerships offer limited income-splitting opportunities, yet provisional tax still applies, as it does with sole proprietors.

All partnerships should have an agreement. An oral one will not do; it should always be in writing. In fact, for best results, a solicitor who is independent of both parties should be used to draw it up. All aspects of the operation and control of the business should be agreed on and should be covered in the Partnership Agreement. Make sure, in particular, that it contains very clear exit clauses and Cessation of Agreement clauses so that each partner is precisely aware of his or her obligations on break-up. In the absence of a written agreement, all partners, whether there are two with fifty per cent each or three with thirty-three per cent or whatever, will always be considered equal. When all's said and done, partnerships are dicey, but if they are properly run, with communication and proper documentation, they can be a highly productive option.

One way to avoid conflict in a partnership is to make the trading activity your only joint investment activity and, indeed, social activity. If you are going to buy other properties or other businesses, or borrow money, do it separately from your partner. Go to different banks, buy your other investments in your own name or in the family name. The problems associated with having all your businesses with the same bank can be horrific if it comes to the need to unwind. The cost, particularly if there is conflict, can undo any profit that might have been achieved.

It comes back to one of the principles of life in general: if something is going well in one situation or with one person, don't try to duplicate it elsewhere. Don't get too familiar with your partner(s). Keep out of each other's pockets. Don't go to

31

the same social functions. Don't go on holidays together. Don't even have the same hobbies. Above all, don't have the same accountant. An accountant cannot be independent when acting for more than one party in a partnership. He or she is likely to be biased towards the partner who brought in the new business. For this reason it is critical to have a separate accountant for each of the partners and one for the entity itself.

A business partner should be chosen with great care. In many ways the requirements are like those for choosing a husband or wife. (Mind you, more waking hours are spent at work than at home.) Therefore, try to imagine living with your prospective partner for the rest of your life. By the same token, your best friend is not necessarily the ideal person to go into business with, because you are likely to be the same sorts of people. Your strengths and weaknesses are likely to be the same, which is counterproductive in business. Consider, for example, two people who are good friends, who play sport and go out socially together. They decide to form a business partnership but they are both salespeople. Unless they employ other people, how can they possibly offset their weaknesses against one another? Although they get on well socially, in business they will probably clash and not give each other value added. If you intend to go into business with another person you should get someone who is good at whatever you are poor at. If you are a salesperson, for example, get someone who is good at finance and accounting or production. Or, if you are not good at selling, get someone who is.

I have seen many successful partnerships formed by people who grew up together — were kids together, went to the same primary school — and went into business when they were aged twenty or so. In such cases there tends to be one dominant personality and they can work together. If they are still working well together by the time they are thirty, their partnership tends to last forever.

Husband/wife partnerships can work, but only if they are very well planned and clear lines are drawn between business and personal issues. Set aside certain times of the day at home when you don't discuss anything to do with the business. This is particularly important when the business has cashflow pressures. Hard times commonly take their toll on marriage/business partnerships.

One of the biggest problems with partnerships is that people keep changing all the time. Personalities change with age, and individual circumstances change, say through divorce or the death of a loved one. A lot of factors can influence the personal basis of the partnership, and this source of potential problems needs to be closely monitored and worked on.

One of the ways to ensure that a partnership works is to get away at least once every twelve months to communicate — thrash out problems, plan the next year, work on your business plan. It need not necessarily be an expensive interstate or overseas holiday. Go for a weekend to a country resort where it is quiet and relaxing, where you are away from the day-to-day hassles of the business and the demands of your family — a place where you can sort out any personality problems in peace and privacy with a bit of relaxation thrown in. One partnership I know meets once a week for dinner. Eight years on, the two partners are still together, they are still growing, they are still successful.

CASE STUDY:

George went into partnership in a small driver training business. Overheads were fairly low, nevertheless they were running five or six leased cars. They had opted for long terms with high residual pay-outs in order to minimise their leasing costs.

Business was going well, until George's wife demanded that he spend more time with her, bring home more money for more trips, let her use one of the business cars, and so on. George's partner, Paul, also started to spend less time in the business, started drawing out more money, starting using the cars for private purposes. The business developed cashflow problems.

One day an almighty blue broke out between George

---

and Paul. But there was no documentation to cover their respective legal rights; they didn't even have a Partnership Agreement. Initially George stayed away and let Paul run the business on his own. Six months later they bumped into each other. Paul said, 'I think I know what's wrong now. I have been taking too much money out of the business and I haven't been working hard enough. The $10,000 overdraft is now $50,000, I am three months behind with lease payments on all the cars and the finance company is threatening to repossess them.' Paul was physically ill and appealed to George for help.

George really had no moral obligation, but he certainly had a financial one. He had two options: to walk away with a debt of $50,000 plus leases — approximately $250,000 worth of liability exposure, or to go back into the business. He went back into the business. He had a meeting with the bank, prepared a business plan with the help of a credible accountant, and asked the creditors for a twelve-month moratorium. Everyone gave George a chance. He worked very hard for the next year and spent little time at home, despite his family problems. He got his overdraft back below $10,000, he re-financed his cars with low residuals and short pay-out periods. He was back on top. But whether George or Paul will ever go into partnership again is another matter.

3 Companies

In legal terms the company is the most complex business structure normally available to small business. Basically it separates the assets and liabilities of the business from those of the individual proprietor. The company therefore becomes a legal entity in its own right. This means it can sue or be sued independently of its officers and directors. More importantly, its members (that is, its shareholders) are limited in their personal liability. If the company goes into liquidation and there are no personal guarantees or other forms of security offered, the shareholders are liable only to the extent of any unpaid capital.

It is important when setting up a company to make sure that any shares issued, no matter how many or to what value, are fully paid. If your business gets into financial trouble, other directors, your creditors and your bank can legally call up the unpaid portion and you are personally liable to pay it.

Companies are the most expensive structure to set up, costing up to $1200 in formation fees, which are not tax deductible. In addition they cost at least $500 a year to administrate. A separate set of taxation returns must be lodged with the Taxation Office and an annual company return with the Australian Securities Commission. This increases the compliance work required by your accountant.

The laws governing the running of companies are becoming more complex and the ASC requirements are increasing, primarily with the intention of protecting the rights of investors.

The company structure should be considered only once the business has been operating for a while and has shown an ability to earn consistent profits. It will protect the proprietor's own personal assets unless personal guarantees or securities are given to banks or creditors. It might also offer some tax advantage in the ability to distribute income to a family trust or related company.

In summary, the *advantages* of a company are:

- Companies can pay dividends. If these dividends are paid from profits from which company taxes will be paid then the shareholder will in effect receive a credit of the company tax which can be offset against the shareholder's liability for personal income tax. This is called dividend imputation, and the dividends in such cases are called franked dividends.
- To some extent, the shareholders have limited liability to creditors, but not for any guaranteed amounts.
- The company has continued life and can be bought and sold.

- The marginal rate for companies is currently lower than it is for individuals and this may create a tax advantage.
- The allowable deduction for superannuation contributed for employees is higher than for sole operators and partners.
- Directors can raise capital by the introduction of additional owners, which will, of course, be easier if the business prospers in the first place and therefore attracts additional investors.

The *disadvantages* are:

- This structure is comparatively expensive to set up and maintain. (Costs might be reduced by using a shelf company and by shopping around for a solicitor to draw up the required legal documents.)
- It is becoming very heavily regulated and costly to operate.
- It is complex to operate and especially to unwind.
- Shareholders do not have complete management control but do have a say in the appointment of directors.
- Directors are legally responsible not only to the shareholders or the owners of the business who appoint them but also to the ASC and to their customers and their creditors or anyone from whom they borrow money. They are subject to numerous government statutory requirements and the onus is on them to ensure the company is trading profitably, otherwise they can be sued personally and can be held personally liable if they continue to trade in the knowledge that the company is unable to meet its commitments.
- Current regulations require that companies choose one of two options for paying tax. The first is to pay 85 per cent of their end-June tax liability (based on the previous year's assessment) by 15 July of the following financial year, and the balance of 15 per

cent upon lodgement (by 15 March of the following financial year). The second option is to pay their full tax liability simultaneously with lodgement, by 15 December of the following financial year.

4 Trusts

A variation of the company structure, and one that is a bit more flexible, is the trust. A trust is simply a vehicle for someone to pledge to look after someone else's money, not unlike a will. The beneficiaries of a trust are like the beneficiaries of a deceased estate. A trust is even more complex to operate and establish than a company and requires that the enterpriser understand his or her obligations under trust law as well as company law. Even if a trust is deemed to be the best vehicle eventually, it should not be adopted until the business's profit potential is fully realised.

A trustee holds the trust property and runs the trust business on behalf of the beneficiary specified in the trust deed. Trusts enable a business's profits to be distributed among any number of beneficiaries, for example, the members of a family, thus reducing the total amount of tax paid.

A trust has no right to act on its own because it is not a legal entity. It can act only via a trustee, which can be a natural person or, indeed, a company. It is more common for companies, rather than individuals, to be appointed as trustees. If the trustee is a company the directors of the company are liable, but if the trustee is an individual he or she is personally liable.

Where high taxable incomes are expected, the discretionary trust structure offers the greatest flexibility for the distribution of income and has tax advantages because you can specify the amounts to go to nominated beneficiaries. Income that goes to unit trust holders such as shareholders of a company, on the other hand, is fixed pro-rata to their unit holding, so you can't necessarily choose between someone who is on a high tax rate and someone who is on a low rate. The Commissioner for Taxation does not allow trusts to be used as income-splitting vehicles in some instances.

To conclude, all options for business structures should be examined, but remember that, when you are first starting off, it is better to keep things simple and keep costs down. If it appears that consistent high profits and significant taxes are going to occur, then more sophisticated and more complicated structures should be considered, such as companies and trusts. However, you are not expected to know all the ins and outs of business structures, particularly from the point of view of tax planning; that is the role of your carefully selected accountant.

PROTECTING YOUR HARD-EARNED WEALTH

The appropriate time to protect your wealth is before you have even accumulated it. It is too late to start doing anything about it when your business is already in financial trouble.

The legal system set up to 'collect' from failed companies is comprehensive and effective, and the courts commonly set aside any elaborate and costly schemes that enterprisers might devise in a last-ditch attempt to save their hard-earned personal assets in the midst of a business collapse. Rather, some simple measures to quarantine assets should be taken while you are setting up your business. Consult a competent lawyer on the details of these.

In the case of a marriage, the partner who runs the business should not be the partner in whose name the family assets are owned. The assets should be held in the name of the spouse or in the name of a separate trust or company. The person owning the assets should not become a director of the company, never sign a personal guarantee and never allow his or her assets to be used as security. He/she must be able to demonstrate that he/she was able to purchase the assets using his/her own income and that the partner involved in the business did not contribute in any way to their purchase.

The sorts of structures that will serve to protect your personal wealth may not always be the most tax effective. But the long-term benefits to yourself and your family should take priority over tax considerations. These structures might also cause some problems in the event of divorce; however, few marriage partners would disagree that it is better to fight over getting less than half of a one-dollar surplus than to be one dollar in debt and have nothing to fight over!

SOME WORDS OF CAUTION

Anyone considering going into business should make him/herself aware of the existence of the Credit Reference Association of Australia (CRAA). This association records the borrowing and payment history of Australian citizens and is available to lenders and certain other authorised entities. It records who has checked you before and whether there have been any defaults or court judgements against you.

This document is of supreme importance. If it contains a nasty little note you will not be able to borrow money and you will have trouble attracting investors. It is very easy to get access to your own report. Just visit the CRAA in your State and fill in an application form, or send them identification details (their telephone number is given at the end of this book). They will then send you any information they have on your file. Any default or judgement entry against you may stay in place for up to five years and the only way to have it removed is to contact the entity that put it there and ask them to do so.

If your report contains any negative information, be honest about it when you are seeking finance or investment. Prepare a written dossier explaining the circumstances of your default and how it was resolved. Get lawyers' and accountants' letters of support as well. Don't try to borrow money hoping that no one will notice your report — especially in difficult times, which call for greater caution on the part of the lender. If everyone was honest in the first place there wouldn't be the need for a CRAA report; in fact, there wouldn't be the need for mortgages. That is why it is so important to confront the situation with complete honesty.

CASE STUDY:

Sarah had a small advertising business. She leased her computer hardware from a finance company linked to the supplier and arranged for her monthly payments to be debited directly to her bank account. When she changed branches and office address mid-term, the direct debit was not transferred by the bank and fell by the wayside. This went unnoticed by Sarah and her accountant until her accountant was contacted by the finance company, who assumed she had gone out of business. The matter was promptly and amicably rectified with a lump sum back payment. In the meantime, however, the finance company had filed a default against Sarah's company; but it was subsequently marked 'paid' and Sarah has since been successful in having the entry removed.

You must also familiarise yourself with the implications of personal guarantees. They are the very shirt off your back. Even when you finance your car you sign a personal guarantee, which literally means that if you can't make a repayment on the due date the financier has the right to come and take the furniture out of your house. Almost everyone in business will be required to sign a personal guarantee sooner or later, especially in hard times. When you lease your premises, when you sign a rental agreement, when you obtain finance from the bank, you will be required to sign a personal guarantee. In most cases you have no alternative, but to retain control you must keep a register of what you have signed. When the various contracts are released, make sure the personal guarantees are released. Make sure you have the contract cancelled and you get a letter to that effect from the financial institution; or if one partner in a partnership is bought out, or you want to sell out yourself, make sure any finance documentation is completely rewritten. Don't rely on third-party letters or indemnities; they are not strong enough and don't give any protection at all.

Finally, a warning: the most common causes of small business failure are failure to plan, inexperience and incompetence. These usually manifest themselves as:

- failure to seek advice, especially financial;
- failure to keep adequate and accurate financial records;
- inadequate market research at the outset;
- deteriorating cashflow and working capital;
- growing too big too fast;
- poor location;
- inadequate promotion and advertising;
- poor knowledge of competition affecting price and marketing policies;
- excessive personal drawings for private use (motor vehicle, holidays);
- failure to maintain cash reserves for contingencies;
- over-extension of credit, excessive overdraft and loans, causing liquidity problems;
- high interest costs;
- financing expansion with interest rates higher than can be earned by the funds borrowed;
- lack of time management;
- failure to insure against possible risks;
- inability to assess a risk and act appropriately;
- inability to motivate employees;
- failure to see trends in macro-economic, social and political concerns, to understand how these might affect the business, and to be flexible enough to be able to benefit from them.

Be aware of these pitfalls and guard against them by continuing to do your research, being careful, keeping your eyes wide open, talking to lots of people, learning as much as you can.

CASE STUDY:

Michael was a very enterprising person with a rural background. The only form of employment he knew was self-employment, but he knew nothing about running a business, small or large, about borrowing, marketing, finance. All he had was an enormous belief in his own ability. At twenty-four he set up his first legal business. He had some innate marketing flair and his business grew rapidly. Clients came from all directions — even from interstate and overseas. Things just kept going from good to better. He never even thought about cashflow, didn't discuss plans, just went with the tide. The economy was booming. Not all his customers paid, but enough money came in to support his lifestyle and business ambitions.

Michael diversified into property investments, convention businesses, marketing businesses, publishing businesses. Within three years he had a whole range of investments, none of which he monitored or followed through. He had a terrible habit of setting up something, getting bored and moving on, without paying any attention to detail. He didn't know what business he was in and he didn't really care, he just wanted to keep growing, feeding his ego, not his bank balance. He was able to present a good case, put some convincing figures down; in fact, he was quite good at borrowing money.

Then the day came when the economy turned. Sales stopped coming in and various partners and directors of the companies he had set up turned against him because things were tough. He had signed numerous guarantees for various rental properties, cars, equipment. He had worked long hours and hadn't paid himself a cent. He had just lived off the businesses and hadn't put away any money. In fact, he had built up some private debt and didn't even realise he was doing it. It had been so easy to borrow. Sure he diversified but none of his investments was returning any money.

Michael eventually came to the realisation that, despite his energy, work ethic and earlier prosperity, things were going rapidly against him. He hadn't paid enough attention to cashflow and profit. There was more cash going out than coming in. He hadn't 'stuck to the knitting', hadn't stayed on course, hadn't concentrated on his legal practice and legal expertise.

Three years down the track, having paid out something like $300,000 in personal guarantees and $200,000 in legal fees, not to mention the price of recriminations, innuendos and threats, he now knows where it's at. He knows what business he's in, concentrates on cashflow, prepares business plans every six months, makes the hard decisions, knows his break-even point, knows exactly what his costs are per month, per week, per day, and has his ego in shape.

When first starting off, by all means have vision but don't have grand schemes. Be modest and careful. In the early stages, the fewer people involved the better, given your limited financial resources. The best time to take on staff or partners is when you are up and running. I believe in doing everything yourself at first, getting your hands dirty, understanding how everything works in your business before employing someone else to do it for you. That way you fully understand what is involved and can keep a hand in it even though you may not be there on a daily basis. Don't think you can come in at the top; in your own business it is better to start at the bottom and work your way up. Basically you should prove yourself to yourself first before even thinking about taking on staff or investors. Starting on your own also keeps the overheads down. It's best to be cautious first, to tread very slowly and carefully.

Small business faces many problems — how to talk to the bank manager, how to handle an irate creditor, whether to buy this way or that way, whether to purchase new equipment, whether to purchase a new car, whether to work longer hours, whether to go on that business trip . . . I have a formula for all these decisions. First, the most important person in your life is yourself and that has implications for your family. So, whatever decision you make on any of these complex issues must be on the grounds of what is best for you and your family. Secondly, consider what is best for cashflow. That means profit, or what is left after the sale has been made. Third and last, consider what's best for tax. Granted, tax is important. But if you have a tax problem you should be pleased, because it means you are making a profit. Make sure you do have a good eye for tax and don't just leave it until the end of the financial year after the horse has bolted. You must constantly monitor the taxation environment because it is always changing, but never let it become a preoccupation in your decision making.

CHAPTER 3

The Business Plan

Every small business must be built on solid ground. Like a tall building, it needs firm foundations to anchor it in strong winds, and the basis of firm foundations is planning. 'To fail to plan is to plan to fail,' as the saying goes.

The ideal approach to general planning is to get away somewhere, safe from all the hassles and constraints and ambitions of your day-to-day life, then just free up your mind and write down what you really want and how you are going to achieve it.

Ask yourself questions like: 'Where do I want to live? How much money do I want to make? How many hours per week do I want to work? How many years do I want to work? What sort of home do I want? What sort of lifestyle do I want? What sort of restaurants do I want to go to? How many holidays do I want to have? What sort of things do I like doing? How much sport do I want to play? Do I want employees; and, if so, how many? What sort of customers do I want? And what will all this cost?'

Write down the answers. Putting things on paper serves to crystallise your thinking. It takes things off your mind, freeing up space which could be used for something else — for remembering something you haven't done, for developing a new idea, or for solving a problem.

Once you have listed your thoughts, you can easily form them into a logical personal plan. I believe that if you don't plan and set goals you are not going to achieve anything. It is just like playing football. Without goals and a strategy for scoring, what is the point of the game? The details (for example, how many hours you want to work) may change from year to year but the overall aims will remain in place.

If you are serious about being successful in business and making money, a business plan is as fundamental to the life of your business as genes are to human biology. In its absence, Simon's Law will prevail: 'Routine drives out planning; the urgent takes priority over the important.' The longer the time taken to develop your business plan, the better it is likely to be. The more you have thought through what can go wrong and what you can do about fixing it, the slimmer the chance that mistakes will occur and the greater your ability to deal with those that do.

The business plan must be cognisant of, and consistent with, the external environment, taking into account economic factors, opportunities and risks; but it must also acknowledge the personal — your current resources and skills, strengths and weaknesses. It is not something you can delegate; it must come from you. Don't say you don't have the time, that you know what the problems are so you don't have to put them on paper, that the job changes from month to month and you cannot plan in advance — that you will wait until things happen and will act accordingly. These are avoidance tactics.

A goal without a plan is a dream. There is plenty of evidence to show that businesses that develop and use formal plans have a greater chance of surviving than those that do not, irrespective of their size — especially in difficult times. The question is not 'Should I plan?' but rather 'How should I go about it?'

THE 'PERFECT' PLAN

The perfect plan is one which helps you achieve your goals and objectives. It passes a 'SWOT' analysis — it capitalises on your Strengths and overcomes your Weaknesses while taking advantage of external Opportunities and, wherever possible, minimising external Threats.

The ideal plan is one that you constantly refer to and review. It is continually changing and evolving, constantly being updated, upgraded and modified to account for changed circumstances — macro and micro. It benefits a number of parties — including staff, banks, customers. (I have twenty plans made up and distributed for a number of different purposes.) At each appropriate stage you should submit the plan to your accountant and other chosen advisers who should prompt you, guide you, encourage you and redirect you in its development.

The business plan is your statement of how you are going to perform in your business. It sets out in detail all your goals and objectives, both personal and professional. It should include market research and analysis and a feasibility study of your planned enterprise. It should also include a marketing plan showing projected sales volume (or number of products or hours of work).

The business plan tells you what production, administrative and personnel facilities you will need to provide the level of turnover budgeted. It tells you what tools of trade are required and in what location. Then it tells you how such a venture will be financed — with how much, in what mix (your own funds and those of investors and lenders) and the equity ratio between each. Clearly, the most important of these is the raising of finance. Going into small business is costly, but finding capital to start up and finance growth is one of the toughest problems the enterpriser faces, especially in times of tight lending policy and high interest rates. It is critical that the business plan identify the exact capital requirements and the correct financing mix.

Once the plan is drawn up it must be discussed amongst the business's owners, directors, advisers and investors. Meetings are held to discuss it, suggestions are made, and the whole thing starts all over again. So, apart from being used by you personally, it should also be used by all those around you, including your senior executives. It is a template for the co-ordination of activity, designed to keep everyone on track and heading in the same direction.

Used outside your operation, the business plan is a vital sales tool. It shows lenders and investors, bankers, customers and suppliers that you and your partners have enough skill and/or experience in your chosen business area to seek opportunities, manage effectively, solve problems and make profits. As such, it should enable you to obtain the custom, credit and finance you desire.

Your plan should cover all the major issues and yet not be so detailed that the reader is turned off. Commonsense should prevail. The guidelines set out in this chapter cover a wide variety of manufacturing and servicing businesses and should not be followed slavishly. For example, a plan for a service business clearly does not require any discussion of manufacturing or product design.

Be realistic in your plan. Start small and keep it simple. Don't have over-ambitious goals. It is better to have lower goals initially so you can get a sense of achievement. Don't stretch yourself to the stage where every last dollar is riding on everything going right. In your decision making and your budgeting and planning always allow for things to go wrong. The plan shouldn't be rushed; it is not something that can be created in a busy day. It might best be achieved during a weekend away with your partners, mentors and/or advisers (see pages 104–110). It then needs sitting on, sleeping on.

Obviously the primary objective in writing a business plan is to shape it for the audience for which it is intended, taking into account the fact that the potential investor/lender is likely initially to devote only five minutes to reading it.

The following pages set out a generic description of what should be included in your plan. It can be adapted to your individual situation, from a simple milk bar operation to a satellite technology business. The end result might be as long as fifty pages or as short as three.

Read and re-read this section. Read it two or three times before commencing your plan and refer to the relevant parts as you go. Answer its questions, be prompted by it, respond to its suggestions and complete your plan accordingly.

THE SUMMARY

A summary at the beginning is critical, and should embody exactly what the potential investors/lenders want to know — through emphasis, not exaggeration or untruths. It should constitute about one tenth of the whole and should give the reader an idea of whether it is worth their while reviewing the rest of the plan carefully.

Write your summary only after you have written your plan. As you draft each section of the plan, highlight a few sentences that you think are important enough to be included in the summary. Allow plenty of time to write the summary. Remember that it is probably the first thing about you and your business that the would-be investor/lender is going to read. Unless it is appealing and convincing, it may also be the last!

Your summary should contain very brief statements about:
1 your business's origins, activities, management and performance;
2 any distinguishing features of your product or service;
3 market attraction;
4 an outline of your financial projections;
5 the amount of money you now seek, in what form (equity or borrowings or both), and for what purpose.

Try to persuade several people to review your summary while it is still in draft form. They should be people, such as your mentor (see pages 109–110), whose business acumen you respect but who are not involved in your venture. Then evaluate their reactions realistically. Did they quickly grasp what you are proposing to do? Were they 'turned on' by what they read? Did they ask you whether they could invest? Their reaction should provide you with some useful indications of how the lender/investor is likely to react.

The summary is then followed by the plan itself, organised along the lines of the following headings:

THE INTRODUCTION

By way of introduction, describe your business and the industry to which it belongs. In this section, you should provide the reader with some background to what you are going to present in subsequent sections about your product/service, your market opportunity, and the people and plans that you have for going after that opportunity. You should briefly describe to whom the product or service is being offered and sketch the nature and current condition of your industry to show where and how you fit into it.

Your Business

Describe the business you are in or intend to enter. Describe your product/services, possible customers, and regions of operation. Trace the history of your business: when it was formed, how its products/services were chosen and developed, and what roles each of the principals has played in bringing the business to where it is today.

If your business is already trading and is now seeking to expand, review its market penetration and its financial performance (sales, profits, return on equity). If, as is to be expected, your business has had early setbacks and incurred losses, describe these and say what you are doing to avoid recurrences. Your proposal might appear too good to be true if you omit all reference to past problems, and these can be readily determined by the reader of the plan from the CRAA (see page 39).

Your Industry

Present your view of the nature, current status and prospects for the industry in which your business operates or will operate. Without going into too much detail, describe in two or three sentences each of the following: the principal participants and how they are performing; growth in sales and profits and also any published forecasts for the current year; companies that have recently entered or left these markets and why; and what major economic, social, technological, or regulatory trends are affecting or are likely to affect your business.

Features and Advantages of Products or Services

The potential banker/investor wants to know exactly what you are going to sell, its proprietary features, if any, and what its advantages and drawbacks are.

Describe, in more detail than previously, the products or services that you sell or intend to sell and what needs they satisfy. Use diagrams, sketches and pictures if these will aid understanding and heighten interest. Emphasise any distinctive features of your product or service by highlighting how it differs from what is currently on the market. State candidly each feature's advantage or disadvantage.

Describe any patents, trade secrets, or other proprietary features. Discuss any head start that you have or could have that would enable you to achieve a favoured or entrenched position in your industry.

Also discuss any opportunities for the logical extension of your existing line or the development of related products or services. Investors like to know what you can do for an encore.

MARKET RESEARCH AND ANALYSIS

In this section of your plan, you should present enough facts to convince the reader that the market for your product or service is such that you can achieve your sales target in the face of competition. This is probably the most difficult section to do well. Yet it is also crucial, simply because choice of marketing strategies, size of work force and facilities, and requirements for inventory and receivables financing are all to be derived from sales forecasts. This section should therefore be prepared before the rest of the plan and should be done very thoroughly.

Customers

Define the market clearly. Explain who are the major purchasers for your product or service, where they are, and why

51

they buy. Discuss and indicate by rank order the significance of price, quality, service, personal contacts, and political pressures. When do they buy? Discuss how seasonal changes affect your business.

List some actual/potential customers who have purchased, expressed interest in or placed an order for your product or service and indicate why. List any actual or potential customers who have dropped, or shown no interest in, your product or service, and explain why this was so. Explain what you are doing to overcome negative customer reaction.

Market Size and Trends

What is the size of the current total market for your product or service? This market should be determined by discussions with potential distributors, dealers, sales representatives, and customers, as well as a review of any available published data. Do not rely solely on published information, as it is often inadequate and known to be so by industry insiders. Give the size of the total market in units as well as dollars. Be careful to include only the market you are in fact going after. If you intend to sell regionally, show the regional market size.

Describe the potential annual growth of the total market for your product or service. Market projections should be made for at least three years. Discuss in more detail than previously how the major factors, such as industry trends, new technical developments, new or changing customer needs, are affecting market growth, and review previous market trends. Any differences between past and projected growth rates should be explained. If you are assuming that past trends will continue, say why. Be aware that overstatement of your market may discredit the rest of your proposal in the eyes of the reader. Information should be sourced to the Bureau of Statistics, employer groups, accountants, industry studies and magazines as appropriate.

Competition

Make a realistic assessment of the strengths and weaknesses of competitive products and services and name the companies that supply them. State the data sources used to determine which products are competitive and the strengths of the competition.

You should compare your products or services with your competitors' on the basis of price, performance, service, warranties, and other pertinent features. A table can be an effective way of presenting such data.

Then review the managerial and financial strengths and weaknesses of your competitors. Give your assessment of each competitor's capability in marketing, operations and finance, and their recent trends in sales, market share and profitability. If they are not doing well, explain why you expect to succeed.

Conclude this section by explaining why customers buy from your three or four key competitors. Then, from what you have presented about their operations, explain why you think that you can capture a share of their business — if that is how you plan to grow.

Enterprisers often know less about their competition than they should, but this is a gross oversight as professional lenders and investors are very wary of proposals that treat competition lightly.

Estimated Market Share and Sales

Identify any major customers who have made or are willing to make purchase commitments. Indicate the extent of these commitments.

Estimate the share of the market and the sales in units and dollars that you think you can achieve. Base this estimate on your assessment of your customers and their acceptance of your product or service, your market size and trends, and the competition, their offerings and their share of sales in the prior year. The growth of your sales and your estimated market share should be related to the growth of your industry and customers and the strengths and weaknesses of your competitors. The data should be presented in tabular form, as shown overleaf. If yours is an existing business, also indicate the total market, your market share, and sales for two prior years.

Sales and market share over two years

| | | SALES AND MARKET SHARE DATA | | | | | | | |
| | | 1ST YEAR | | | | 2ND YEAR | | | |
		Q1	Q2	Q3	Q4	Q1	Q2	Q3	Q4
Estimated total market	Units								
	Dollars								
Your estimated sales	Units								
	Dollars								
Your estimated market share	Units								
	Dollars								

THE MARKETING PLAN

Your marketing plan should describe how you will achieve your sales target. It should include a description of your sales and service policies as well as pricing, distribution and advertising strategies that you will use to achieve your goal, and should make clear what is to be done, how it will be done, and who will do it.

Marketing Strategy

A description of your marketing strategy (see pages 167–177) should include a discussion of the kinds of customers who will be targeted for an initial heavy selling effort, customers who will be sought for later selling efforts, the method of identifying and contacting specific potential customers, and the features of the product or service (quality, price, delivery, warranty) that will be emphasised to generate sales.

If the sales of your product or service are seasonal, discuss this and indicate any ideas you have for obtaining out-of-season sales.

Pricing

Many enterprisers, having convinced prospective investors that they have a superior product, say they intend to sell it for less than their competitors. This makes a bad impression for two reasons. First, if your product is as good as you say it is, you should not have to undercut the competition. Secondly, if you use low prices as a marketing drawcard you have no room for manoeuvring. At least if you start at a higher price and costs run over budget, as they usually do, you have some scope to come down. Price hikes are tougher to make stick than price cuts.

As we will see in chapter 6, your pricing policy is one of the more important decisions you make. Your price must be right to penetrate your market, maintain your market position, and produce the profits you project. Devote enough time to considering a number of pricing strategies and convincingly present the one you select.

Discuss the prices to be charged for your product or service and compare your pricing policy with those of your major competitors. Explain how the price you set will enable you to:

- secure/increase acceptance of your business opportunity;
- maintain and desirably increase your market share in the face of competition;
- produce profits.

Justify any price increases over competitive items on the basis of newness, quality, warranty and service. If your product is to be priced lower than your competitors' products explain how you will do this without losing profitability.

Sales Tactics

Describe how you will sell and distribute your product or service. Do you or will you use your own sales force and distributors? Are there ready-made manufacturers' sales organisations selling related products that you already use or could use? If distributors or sales representatives are used, describe how they have been or will be selected, and the areas they will cover. Discuss the margins to be given to retailers and wholesalers, and your commissions to sales representatives, and compare them to those given by your competition. Describe any special policies regarding items such as discounts and exclusive distribution rights.

If a direct sales force is being introduced, indicate how it will be organised and at what rate it will be built up. Show the sales expected per salesperson per year and what commission incentive and/or salary they will receive. Explain how these figures compare to those of your competition.

Service and Warranty Policies

If your business will offer a product that will require service and warranties, indicate the importance of these to the customer's purchasing decision and discuss your method of handling service problems.

Advertising, Public Relations and Promotion

Describe the programme you will use to bring your product to the attention of prospective customers. Indicate your plans for public relations, trade show participation, trade magazine advertisements, direct mailings, and the preparation of product sheets and promotional literature. If advertising will be a significant part of company expenses, present details of how and when these costs will be incurred.

DESIGN AND DEVELOPMENT

If any of your products or services require design and development before they are ready to go on the market, the nature and extent of this work should be fully discussed. The costs and time required to achieve a marketable product or service should be indicated.

Such design and development might be the engineering work necessary to convert a laboratory prototype to a finished product; the design of special tooling; the work of an industrial designer to make a product more attractive and saleable; or the identification and organisation of manpower, equipment, and special techniques. Or it might be to implement a service business — for example, the equipment, new computer software, and skills required for computerised credit checking.

Development Status and Tasks

Describe the current status of the product or service and explain what remains to be done to make it marketable. Describe briefly the competence or expertise that your business has, or will acquire, to complete this development. Indicate the type and extent of technical assistance that will be required, state who will supervise this activity within your organisation, and give his or her experience in related development work.

Difficulties and Risks

Identify any major anticipated design and development problems and ways of solving these. Discuss their possible impact on the timing of the market introduction of your product or service and the cost of design and development.

Costs

Present and discuss a design and development budget. The costs should include labour, materials, consulting fees, and so on. Design and development costs are often underestimated. This can have a serious impact on cashflow projections. Accordingly, consider and perhaps show a ten- to twenty-per-cent cost contingency. These cost data will become an integral part of the financial plan.

PRODUCTION/OPERATIONS

The operations plan should describe the kind of facilities, space requirements, capital equipment, and labour force (part and full time) that are required to deliver the forecast quantities of the company's product or service (see pages 114–123). For a manufacturing business, discuss your policies regarding purchasing, 'make or buy' decisions (which parts of the products will be purchased and which operations will be performed by your work force), inventory control, and production control. A service business should describe the appropriateness of location, lease of required equipment, and competitive productivity from a skilled or trained labour force.

The discussion guidelines given below are general enough to cover both product and service businesses. Only those that are relevant to your business type should be used in preparing the business plan.

Geographic Location

Describe the location of the business and discuss any advantages and disadvantages of the site in terms of wage rates, unions, labour availability, closeness to customers or suppliers, access to transportation, State and local taxes, Federal, State and local laws, utilities, and zoning. For a service business, proximity to customers is generally a 'must'.

Facilities and Improvements

If the business already exists, describe the facilities currently used to conduct it. This should include plant and office space, storage and land areas, machinery, special tooling, and other capital equipment.

If you are starting up your own venture, describe how and when the necessary facilities to start production will be acquired. Discuss whether equipment and space will be leased or acquired (new or used), and indicate the costs and timing of such actions.

58

Indicate how much of the proposed financing will be devoted to plant and equipment.

Discuss how and when plant space and equipment will be moved or expanded to the capacities required to achieve future sales projections. Explain future equipment needs and indicate the timing and cost of any acquisitions. A three-year planning period should be used for these projections.

Production Strategies

Describe the manufacturing processes involved in producing your goods and any decisions with respect to subcontracting component parts rather than manufacturing them in-house. The 'make or buy' strategy adopted should consider inventory financing, available labour skills and other non-technical questions as well as pure production, cost and capability issues. Justify your proposed 'make or buy' policy. Discuss any surveys you have completed of potential subcontractors and suppliers and name these.

Present a production plan that shows cost-volume information at various levels of operation with breakdowns of applicable material, labour, purchased components and factory overheads. Discuss the inventory required at various sales levels. These data will be incorporated into cashflow projections (see pages 66–8 and chapter 6). Explain how any seasonal production loads will be handled without severe dislocation — for example, by building up inventory, using part-time help or subcontracting the work.

Briefly describe your approach to quality control, production control and inventory control. Explain what quality control and inspection procedures the company will use to minimise service problems and associated customer dissatisfaction.

Discuss how you will organise and operate your purchasing function to ensure that adequate materials are on hand for production, that the best price and payment terms have been obtained, and that raw materials and in-process inventory (and hence working capital) have been minimised.

Labour Force

Explain, exclusive of management functions (discussed below), to what extent the local labour force has the necessary skills in sufficient quantity and quality (lack of absenteeism, productivity) to manufacture the product or supply your business's services to whatever standards of quality, time and cost you have established. If the skills of the labour force are inadequate for the needs of your business, describe the kinds of training that you will use to upgrade them. Discuss how your business can provide and pay for such training and still offer a competitive product in both the short term (first year) and the long term (two to five years).

Management Team

The management team is the key to a successful business. Investors look for a committed management team with a balance in marketing, operations and financial skills and experience in doing what is proposed.

Accordingly, this section of the business plan will be of primary interest to potential investors and will significantly influence their investment decisions. It should include a description of the key members of the management team and their primary duties, the organisation structure, and the board of directors. The reputation and strength of at least one independent director will be critical when seeking finance or investors.

Organisation

In a table, present the key management roles in the company and name the person holding each position.

Discuss any current or past situations in which the key management people have worked together that indicate how their skills and personalities complement each other and result in an effective management team. If any key individuals will not be on hand at the start of the venture, specify when they will join the company or what you are doing to locate and secure commitments from such individuals. In a new business, it may not be possible to fill each executive role with a full-time person without excessively burdening the overheads of the venture. One solution is to use part-time specialists or consultants to perform some functions. If this is your plan, discuss it and indicate who will be used and when they will be replaced by a full-time staff member.

If the company is established and of sufficient size, an organisation chart can be appended as an exhibit.

Executive Management Personnel

Describe the exact duties and responsibilities of each of the executive members of the management team. Include a brief (three- or four-sentence) statement of the career highlights of each individual to focus on accomplishments that demonstrate ability to perform the assigned role.

Complete résumés for each valued management member should be included here or as an appendix to the business plan. These résumés should stress education, training, experience and accomplishments of each person in performing functions similar to that person's role in the venture. Accomplishments should be discussed in terms of profit and sales improvement, labour productivity gains, reduced operating costs, improved product performance, and ability to meet budgets and schedules. When possible, it should be noted who can attest to accomplishments and recognition or rewards received, such as pay increases and promotions.

Management Compensation and Ownership

The likelihood of obtaining financing for a start-up is small when the founding management team is not prepared to accept modest initial salaries. If you demand substantial salaries in excess of what you received at your prior employment, the potential lender/investor will conclude that your psychological commitment to the venture is a good deal less than it should be. In hard times lenders and investors take a particularly dim view of actual or perceived abuses in the area of remuneration.

State the salary that is to be paid to each valued person and compare it with the salary received at her or his last independent job. Set forth the share ownership planned for the valued management team members, the amount of their equity investment (if any), and any performance-dependent option or bonus plans that are contemplated. Mention any loans made to the company by management, indicating on what terms they were made and under what circumstances they can be converted to equity.

Board of Directors

Identify board members and include a one- or two-sentence statement of each member's background to show how he or she can benefit the company and what investment (if any) has been made. Include the résumé of the independent board member, showing any other directorships.

Management Assistance and Training Needs

Describe candidly the strengths and weaknesses of your management team and board of directors. Discuss the kind, extent and timing of any management training that will be required to overcome any weaknesses.

Supporting Professional Services

State the legal, accounting, public relations, advertising, banking, and other service organisations that you have selected for your venture. Supporting service organisations that are reputable and capable (remember reputations often live on after capability diminishes) not only provide professional assistance, but can also add significantly to the credibility of your business. In addition, properly selected professional organisations can help you establish good contacts in the business community, identify potential investors and secure finance. Also mention your mentor if you have one (see pages 109–110).

OVERALL SCHEDULE

A schedule that shows the timing and interrelationship of the major events necessary to launch the business and realise its objectives is an essential part of a business plan. In addition to being a planning aid, a well-prepared and realistic schedule can be an extremely effective sales tool in raising money from potential bankers/investors. It also demonstrates the ability of the management team to plan for venture growth in a way that recognises obstacles and minimises risk.

Prepare, as a part of this section, a month-by-month schedule that shows the timing of activities such as product development, market planning, sales programmes, and operations. Sufficient detail should be included to show the timing of the primary tasks required to accomplish each major goal.

Show on the schedule the deadlines or milestones critical to the venture's success. These should include:

- incorporation of the new business;
- completion of prototypes (this is a key date as its achievement is a tangible measure of the company's ability to perform);
- when sales representatives are obtained;
- date of displays at trade shows;
- when distributors and dealers are signed up;
- ordering materials in sufficient quantities for full-time operation;
- start of operation (this is another key date because it is related to the production of income);
- receipt of first orders;
- first sales and deliveries (this is a date of maximum interest because it relates directly to the company's credibility and need for capital);
- payment of first accounts receivable (cash in).

The schedule should also show the following and their relation to the development of the business:

- number of management personnel;
- number of operations personnel;
- additions to plant or equipment.

CRITICAL RISKS AND PROBLEMS

The development of a business has risks and problems, and the business plan invariably contains some implicit assumptions about them. Credibility can be undermined and finance endangered if negative factors are not openly addressed. On the other hand, identifying and discussing the risks in your venture demonstrates your skill as a manager and increases your credibility with a banker/investor. Taking the initiative to identify and discuss risks helps you demonstrate to the lender/investor that you have thought about them and can handle them. Risks then tend not to loom as large black clouds in the lender's/investor's thinking.

Accordingly, identify and discuss the major problems and risks that you think you will have to deal with to develop your venture. Include a description of the risks relating to your industry, your company and its personnel, your product's market appeal, and the timing and financing of your start-up. Among the risks that might require discussion are the following:

- price cutting by competitors;
- any potentially unfavourable industry-wide trends;
- design or operating costs significantly in excess of estimates;
- development schedule not met;
- sales projections not achieved by target date;
- difficulties or long lead times encountered in the procurement of parts or raw materials;
- difficulties encountered in obtaining needed bank credit lines because of tight money;
- larger-than-expected innovation and development costs to stay competitive;
- lack of availability of trained labour;
- change in the economy;
- higher interest rates.

This list is by no means comprehensive but only indicative of the kinds of risks and assumptions involved.

Show which business plan assumptions or potential problems are most critical to the success of the venture. Describe your plans for minimising the impact of unfavourable developments in each risk area on the success of your venture.

THE FINANCIAL PLAN

The financial plan is basic to any lender's/investor's evaluation of your business and should represent your realistic and best estimates of future operations. Its purpose is to indicate the financial potential of your enterprise and its capital needs. The financial plan should also serve as an operating plan for financial management of the business.

In developing your financial plan, three basic statements must be prepared:

- profit and loss forecasts for three years;
- cashflow projections for three years;
- pro forma balance sheets at start-up, semi-annually in the first year, and at the end of each of the first three years of operation.

In the case of an existing business seeking expansion capital, balance sheets and income statements for the current and two prior years should be presented in addition to these finance projections.

After you have completed the preparation of the financial exhibits, briefly outline the important conclusions that can be drawn. This might include items such as the maximum cash requirement, the amount to be supplied by investors and debt, the level of profits as a percentage of sales, and how fast any borrowings are to be repaid.

Profit and Loss Forecast

The preparation of your business's projected income statements is the planning-for-profit part of your financial plan. Crucial to the earnings forecasts, as well as other projections, is

65

the sales forecast. The methods for developing sales forecasts have already been described in these guidelines, and the sales forecasts made there should be used here.

The following headings can be used in drawing up your profit and loss forecast for prospective investors.

Sales
    Less: Materials used
    Direct labour
    Manufacturing overheads
    (includes rent, utilities, fringe benefits, telephone)
    Other manufacturing expense, leased equipment, and
    so on
    Depreciation
    Total cost of goods sold
Gross profit (or loss)
    Less: Sales expenses
    General and administrative expenses, office supplies,
    accounting and legal services, management, and so on

Operating profit (or loss)
    Less: Other expenses (e.g. interest)
Profit (or loss) before taxes
Income tax provision
Profit (or loss) after taxes

The first year should show a monthly breakdown for each item. The second and third years should project quarterly figures. Figures for all three years should appear on a single sheet of ruled paper — make sure the paper you use is large enough. Tape two pages together if necessary.

Once the sales forecasts are in hand, production costs (or operations costs for a service business) should be budgeted. The level of production or operation that is required to meet the sales forecasts and also to fulfil inventory requirements must be determined. The material, labour, service and manufacturing overhead requirements must be developed and translated into cost data.

Sales expenses should include the costs of selling and distribution, storage, discounts, and advertising and promotion. General and administrative expenses should include management salaries, secretarial costs, and legal and accounting expenses. Manufacturing or operations overheads includes items such as rent, utilities, fringe benefits and telephone.

Because of the importance of profit and loss projections, you should explain any assumptions that you made in their preparation. Such assumptions could include the amount allowed for bad debts and discounts, and sales expenses or general and administrative costs as a fixed percentage of costs or sales.

Cashflow Forecast

For a new business, the cashflow forecast can be more important than the forecasts of profits because it details the amount and timing of expected cash inflows and outflows. Usually the level of profits, particularly during the formative years of a business, will not be sufficient to finance operating cash needs. Moreover, cash inflows do not match the outflows on a short-term basis. The cashflow forecast will indicate these conditions.

The cashflow forecast records *all* cash receipts and payments, including those which do not appear in the profit and loss statement — for example, the capital portion of loan payments. It does not record expenses which do not affect the flow of cash or profits, such as depreciation and provision for bad debts. In preparing the cashflow budget it is important to know or estimate both the *amount* of the income/expense to be received/paid and *when* it will occur. The purpose of this document is to predetermine the timing and size of shortfalls or surpluses, so that steps can be taken to arrange additional funds to be raised or invested as appropriate. If a continuous or increasing cash shortfall is forecast, a more permanent source of capital should be considered — for example, increased owners' equity or a longer term loan. The cashflow forecast should allow for actual income/payments to be inserted so that a comparison can be made with estimates.

Like the income statement, the cashflow analysis should cover three years, with the first year broken down into twelve monthly figures and the second and third years projected by quarters. Again, this analysis should be made on a single large sheet of ruled paper. The following headings can be used in preparing the analysis:

Bank balance: Opening (debit or credit)

ADD cash receipts
  Collection of debtors/cash sales
  Sundry receipts
  Bank loans
  Capital contributed
    Total receipts

LESS cash payments
  Creditors
  Wages
  Manufacturing overheads
  Leased equipment
  Sales expenses
  General and administrative expenses
  Fixed asset purchases
  Income tax
  Loan interest @ _____%
  Loan repayments
  Sundry payments
    Total disbursements

EQUALS cash surplus (or deficit)

Bank balance: Closing (debit or credit)

Given a level of projected sales and capital expenditures over a specified period, the cashflow forecast will highlight the need for, and timing of, additional financing and show you your peak requirements of working capital. You must decide how this additional finance is to be obtained, on what terms, and how it is to be repaid (see chapter 4). Part of the needed financing will be supplied by yourself, your family and friends, by contacts and by professional investors; part by bank loans for one to five years; and the balance by short-term lines of credit from banks. This information becomes part of the final cashflow forecasts.

If the venture is in a seasonal or cyclical industry, in an industry in which suppliers require a new firm to pay cash, or if an inventory build-up occurs before the product can be sold and produce revenues, the cashflow forecast is crucial to the continuing operation of your business. A detailed cashflow forecast that you understand can enable you to direct your attention to operating problems without the distractions caused by periodic cash crises that you should have anticipated.

You should discuss assumptions made on the timing of collection of debtors, discounts given, terms of payments to your suppliers, planned salary and wage increases, anticipated increases in any operating expenses, seasonal characteristics of the business as they affect inventory requirements, and capital equipment purchases. Thinking about such assumptions when planning the operation of your business is useful for identifying issues that may later require attention if they are not to become significant problems.

Balance Sheet Forecasts

The balance sheet is used to show the assets required in the operation of your business and, through liabilities, how these assets are to be financed. Investors and bankers look to the projected balance sheet for information such as debt-to-equity ratios, working capital, current ratios, and inventory turnover. The lenders/investors will relate them to the acceptable limits required to justify future financings that are projected for the venture.

The following headings may be used to prepare the balance sheet forecasts:

ASSETS
Current assets
   Cash
   Debtors
   Stock
   Prepayments

Total current assets

Non-current assets
   Plant and equipment
   Less: Accumulated depreciation
   Net plant and equipment
   Land and buildings
   Other assets (identify)

Total assets

LESS LIABILITIES
Current liabilities
   Loans
   Creditors
   Accruals
   Taxes
   Other

Total current liabilities

Non-current liabilities
   Long-term loans
   Other liabilities (identify)

Total liabilities

EQUALS SHAREHOLDERS' (PARTNERSHIP) FUNDS
   Paid-up capital
   Retained profits

   Total shareholders' (partnership) funds

Forecast balance sheets should be prepared at start-up, semi-annually for the first year, and at the end of each of the first three years of operation.

Cost and Cashflow Control

Your ability to meet your income and cashflow projections will depend critically on your ability to secure timely reports on, and effectively control, your operating costs. For this reason, bankers and investors will want to know what kind of cost-control systems you have or will use in your business. The financial plan should include a brief description of how you will design, install and maintain systems for controlling costs and cashflows appropriate to the nature and size of your business, who will be responsible for getting cost data, how often cost data will be obtained and how you will take action to reduce costs that are running higher than you expected.

Desired Financing

Summarise from your cashflow projections how much money you will need over the next three years to carry out the development and expansion of your business as described. Indicate how much of this money you expect to obtain now from your own resources and investors and how much you think you can borrow. Describe the kind (ordinary shares, convertible notes, debentures), the unit price and the total amount of equity to be issued to investors. Also show the percentage of the company that investors in this offering will hold after the offering is completed and what special rights they will have.

Capitalisation

Show in a table the names of your current shareholders and the number of shares each holds. Also indicate how many of your company's ordinary shares will remain authorised but unissued.

Use of Funds

Bankers and investors like to know how their money is going to be spent. Provide a brief description of how the capital raised will be used. Summarise as specifically as possible what amount will be used for such things as product development, capital equipment, marketing, and general working capital needs.

71

CASE STUDY:

Wayne and Jenny were two friends who had known each other for some twenty years, since school. They had each worked for a number of graphic design and photographic studios for four or five years, and at the ripe old age of twenty-four they decided to go into business together.

They had been going along quite nicely for about twelve months, with a very small office, a slide-making machine and a computer graphics package. The whole set-up had cost them no more than $40,000. They developed a good-quality client base and were basically running a small, tight, profitable business. They met regularly, and even went out to dinner every Thursday night without their spouses just to discuss business matters. The only problem they had was trying to get good-quality staff.

They each wanted to buy their own home and had decided to purchase two slide computer machines at a total cost of $300,000. This meant that, collectively, they were borrowing something like $800,000. They approached my company to prepare a business plan. With guidance from us they wrote their own plan with all the required elements: clearly stated goals and objectives; a great deal of market research, statistics and studies; a marketing plan that was simple, logical and easy to carry out; clear documentation of equipment, facilities and location; very detailed cashflows and budgeting; and the exact financial requirements, with their contribution and the borrowing mix.

Although we knew the plan was ambitious we submitted it to three financiers, one being a traditional bank, one being a finance company and the other being an entrepreneurial venture company. Within a week all three had approved the finance and the managing director of the finance company sought aggressively to acquire a half share in the business.

Jenny and Wayne were able to choose their financier and also had the option of taking on a partner who would inject capital, thereby reducing worry, risk and interest. They deliberated over the next two days and came back to me, against my advice, with the decision to go it alone. They had made the right decision. Four years later they have stuck rigidly to their plan, they haven't taken on any major changes or increased commitments. They are achieving the profits they said they would and they are rapidly reducing their debt, they are still meeting every Thursday night, they are still reviewing their figures, they know exactly what their costs are and their break-even point. And they have their staff problem under control.

PRESENTING YOUR PLAN

Presenting the business plan that you have so carefully and painstakingly prepared should not be a daunting experience. On the contrary, it should be your moment of glory, your reason to feel proud.

As mentioned earlier, a number of people should be presented with a copy of the plan, but we will concentrate here on prospective lenders. Some straightforward rules apply (and these also hold good for potential investors).

First, before making contact with your chosen financier make sure you understand every aspect of the plan. If you have prepared it according to the above guidelines, this shouldn't cause any problems, except perhaps if it contains difficult financial information. If the accountant prepared it, perhaps you should invite her/him to join you at the meeting. Familiarise yourself with every word, every figure, to such an extent that you will not need to refer to the report during your interview.

Next, find out from your lending institution who is the person with relevant authority. This will avoid wasting time — yours and theirs. Then make an appointment to see them, explaining the purpose of your intended visit. Send a copy of your plan in advance with an agenda for discussion.

Be on time for your interview. Dress cleanly and tidily, in a suit or equally businesslike outfit (jeans are definitely out). Even if wearing such attire is not usual for you, show flexibility in adapting to the conventions of different environments, in this case that of the commercial lender. On the other hand, don't overdress. Your aim is to convey a professional and capable image. Consider having your spouse or business partner accompany you to the interview to show support and commitment.

In addition to your copy of the business plan take all available financial statements and projections, having had these checked by your accountant (or having had them prepared by your accountant if you don't have the skills). Also take any relevant statistics, survey data, maps and analyses and offer copies to the bank manager. (Believe it or not, many banks don't have photocopiers!)

Let the bank's (or lender's or investor's) representative do most of the talking to start with, giving you time to relax and prepare yourself. When you do speak, do so slowly and clearly. Be neither vague nor overpowering. Be enthusiastic but don't push for a decision. The lender/investor will need time to think about the interview and to some extent will be guided by your performance at it. Inspire her/him with your confidence and your ability to run the business, repay the loan and return a profit on the investment.

Behave professionally; show that you are serious and capable of running an efficient and profitable business. Treat your prospective lender/investor with respect. When you present your business plan you are selling your business, your professionalism, your expertise, your commitment, and in exchange you are looking to buy their product — money. The first impression that you create as a person will be a lasting one. Conduct yourself with your lenders and investors just as you do with your customers and creditors. It is very important that you be honest and communicate openly. Be realistic: don't ignore the negative side of the picture. Be frank. The lender/investor will place great store on your honesty, so answer any questions candidly and completely. You can be certain that you won't get a loan if you raise suspicion that you are holding back information. Apart from protecting your own reputation and your long-term relationship with the lender/investor, you want to enhance your chances of obtaining further loans or investment funds if needed or being able to come back later if the first application is declined.

If your request is declined find out why and what you have to do to correct the reason for the knock-back. This will enable you to revamp the business plan to meet the criteria given. Don't give in, even after three or four rejections. If you have properly prepared your plan and believe in it, you needn't feel perturbed, particularly when money is tight and the banks are taking a long time to make up their minds and are imposing increasingly stringent requirements. Unfortunately in these hard times many good bank managers have been shifted upstairs into recovery because of the increased number of bad debts, or they have been transferred from branch to branch to ensure that they maintain their detachment. The banks' senior executives are putting a lot of pressure on managers with regard to the high number of non-performing loans. That is why managers may be slightly negative at the moment and also why you need to shop around.

Just keep making approaches until you find the ideal mix with a lender or investor who suits you. Two of the biggest companies in the United States — Digital, and Research and Development — were knocked back by many lenders and investors before they got going.

Remember: a good business plan is one that raises money. A bad plan does not attract investors and does not raise money. That fact is simple enough, but it should also be noted that a good plan does not create a good business. A good plan may raise money, yet the business may still fail. However, a bad plan always leads to a failed business. To succeed you need a good plan plus a good business.

CHAPTER 4

Raising Finance

F inance is often the major cost to any small business other than salaries (which will be discussed later). When interest rates are relatively low this cost can usually be carried without too much effort, but when rates are high it tends to decrease the fair return for efforts or even to send businesses broke.

Wherever possible it is best to avoid using other people's money to finance your business. Ideally the business should be self-financing — that is, the profit should be its source of finance. When you are making profits, you are putting money back into your business, increasing your working capital (i.e. stock, debtors) and increasing your profits in the future. Money earned by the business is the best and cheapest source of finance. It does not incur interest and does not have to be repaid, it's totally controllable — it can't be taken from you — and you don't have to sign any guarantees or put up any security for it. If your business is just beginning and is expanding rapidly you are forced to maintain an increased sales volume to meet the increasing overhead costs. Often a slower rate of progress is better, making costs easier to control and operations more profitable even if the total sales are down, and thus minimising the need to borrow. After all, you should be interested only in net profit and not expansion for the sake of expansion.

However, your ability to expand or to take advantage of an opportunity will often depend on an injection of funds from external sources. Even if you have funds available from internal sources, it might still be a good idea to start looking for outside money long before you have fully used all your own. If you do this, do you want equity capital from investors or debt capital from a finance company or bank, or perhaps both?

Equity capital means selling off part of your business by taking on a partner or selling shares. Before investing, investors would wish to peruse your business plan. Let's say your business is worth $400,000 net (including stock and goodwill) and you are prepared to divest yourself of forty per cent in order to retain the majority of the shares. The contribution from investors would then be $160,000 (40% x $400,000). In order for that capital to remain in the business you would need to lend that money back to the business on agreed terms, because really you are selling shares that belonged to you. When you do this there is less pressure to repay the funds. However, possible disincentives are that you lose exclusive control of your business and you may introduce the partnership problems discussed in chapter 2.

When considering borrowing you will need to take into account three factors: the cost, the availability and the terms. Shop around for the deal that suits you in all these respects. Make sure the term of the loan matches the purpose for which it is intended: always borrow short to invest short and borrow long to invest long; to borrow short and invest long is one of the steepest paths to the business grave.

Bank overdraft is the most popular type of finance sought by small businesses as it is the most flexible. Although you will be charged a line fee which is tied to the approved limit of the overdraft, you will pay interest only on what you use and the rate will vary according to the market and the status of your business.

Excessive dependence on a bank overdraft (in principle, repayable on demand) is dangerous, particularly in the eyes of other prospective suppliers of finance. If you do have an overdraft, make sure you trade it up and down to the top and bottom levels, even if you have to swap cheques backwards and forwards. Don't sit on your approved limit, or it will be considered a poor debt and the bank might either force you to pay it back or swap it for a higher, fixed-interest loan with additional security. Cyclical requirements can be serviced by commercial bills, on which interest is charged up-front and which are repayable in full on maturity. Another form of finance is a short-term loan — say, for twelve to eighteen months. Long-term funding comes from various sources, such as long-term business loans, fully drawn advances (FDAs) or fixed loans. Secu-

The following chart is a guide to types and main sources of funds:

SHORT-TERM DEBT FINANCE — up to 3 years (including temporary working capital; bridging finance; funds to meet seasonal fluctuations; finance for short-term assets)	MEDIUM-TERM DEBT FINANCE — 3–10 years (including finance for assets with medium-term life, e.g. plant and machinery, general working capital, overdraft funding)	LONG-TERM DEBT FINANCE — more than 10 years (including finance for long-life assets, e.g. buildings, corporate acquisitions)	OWNER'S/ INVESTORS' EQUITY CAPITAL (including permanent capital, e.g. for technological innovation, for development and expansion, for the refinancing of borrowings)
trading banks	trading banks	trading banks	family/friends
savings banks	savings banks	savings banks	accountants/ lawyers
Commonwealth Development Bank	Commonwealth Development Bank	Commonwealth Development Bank	merchant banks/ money market corporations
merchant banks/money market corporations	finance companies	merchant banks/ money market corporations	life insurance offices
finance companies		finance companies	superannuation funds
		church groups	Australian Industry Development Corporation
		life insurance offices	stockbrokers
		non-life insurance companies	venture capital companies
		superannuation funds	private individuals
		debt raisings	

rity is usually required against all bank finance and suitability depends on your cashflow.

Remember that there is no point in changing your borrowings from bank to bank as it may cost you in stamp duty and legal fees as well as time taken up in negotiating, meeting and preparing documentation. The banks are wise to such manoeuvrings, anyway.

In all your business dealings never lose sight of the twin spectres of under-capitalising and over-trading. These horrors often go together because, although they do not mean quite the same thing, they stem from a common source.

The trading entity is rather like an upturned pyramid with the sales represented by the upper horizontal line and the capital by the bottom point. If the point is too weak to support the remainder it will topple over into bankruptcy or the liquidation courts.

Under-capitalisation can lead to inadequate supplies of materials and consequent disruption to production and delivery, lost opportunities and expensive buying procedures. An over-ambitious business may follow a policy of going for increased sales volume, and over-trading is likely to ensue. Outside borrowing is increased until a stage is reached where an inability to meet interest and capital repayments forces a showdown.

Never allow your business to reach even the margin of these deadly shores. One way to check on safety is a method known as capital gearing, that is, the ratio of borrowed funds to your own money. Every business is different and circumstances have some bearing on individual cases. Even so, the ideal ratio for a business is usually determined by the norm for that particular industry. In general, the greater the degree of risk attached to a particular type of business, the lower the desirable gearing ratio. A sound balance sheet usually shows a capital ratio of not more than 1:2, that is, your equity is at least twice borrowings. For small businesses the ratio 1:1 would be the maximum gearing ratio which could be attempted without encountering criticism, except where there are temporary or special factors.

Where a business's gearing approaches the higher end of its normal range it should be taken as a danger signal, that is, a strong sign that a further equity injection is becoming desirable, if not essential. Neither the lender's nor the owner's interests are served by borrowings that are too high. A business in a highly geared position applying to borrow funds for further expansion can expect the lender to require an injection of the borrower's own money or equity finance as a condition of lending, quite possibly of a greater amount than that being lent. In the eyes of the lender the equity base represents the owner's commitment to the business; and the greater the commitment, the more likely the lender's willingness to help. Lack of equity or one's own money in small business would normally necessitate personal guarantees by shareholders and directors.

The chief dangers of high capital gearing are quite simple: the burden of interest payments and any scheduled debt repayments will become too great in relation to the earnings and cashflow available to meet them. Also, a business with such a limited cash equity base will be unable to cushion or absorb the impact of suddenly adverse trading conditions. One useful test of the capacity to service debt repayments is whether the net trading profits before interest and tax cover the total of all interest charges at least twice over.

You should note that ASC restrictions apply to the seeking of investors/equity. Any offers to the public, if considered a 'prescribed interest', require a prospectus. This topic is not germane to this book but nevertheless it is critical that you understand it. Advice should be sought from your accountant and/or solicitor.

ROMANCING THE BANKERS

When you approach your bank — be it to borrow or to invest — always show courtesy and respect. Don't turn up with your figures on scraps of paper. Your bank manager is a busy person and you will be welcome only if you make an effort to communicate clearly and efficiently.

When considering applications for finance, banks are interested in three things. Firstly, they look at your *reputation*, your track record — that is, how you have conducted yourself in the past in dealing with lending and investing institutions; and your standing in the business community, amongst your peers and competitors. Secondly, they look at *cashflow* from the business — that is, your ability to repay the loan, which should be included in your business plan. Indicate clearly how you will be able to afford the commitments you are taking on, whether they are interest commitments or repayments of dividends or share of profit to potential investors, and how comfortably you will be able to do that while at the same time maintaining your business growth and your lifestyle. Banks and investors don't want to have bad debts, they don't want to sell you up; they prefer to make sure that you can pay them back or you can return a profit to them on their invested dollars. It is handy to note that bank managers are paid a wage which is contingent upon their performance, and that performance has a number of criteria. Obviously, any bad debts or bad loans affect their performance and chances for promotion. On the other hand, good loans, good debts and good customers enhance their income. They like to see you actively trading your account, into and out of overdraft.

Finally, particularly in these hard economic times, the banks are interested in *security*. The bank considers some or all of the following as security or collateral: mortgage over real estate, floating charges over the assets of your business, bills of sale over the fittings and plant owned by the business, and guarantees of different types. In the case of a company, bankers will usually request a real estate security and personal guarantees from directors. They may also seek a charge over the company's assets. Banks make their own valuations of assets and determine their lending on that basis. In hard times, though, most lenders will look only at bricks and mortar, and then they cut back on lending values. As a guide, on houses they will lend up to 60 or 70 per cent, sometimes higher with mortgage insurance, and with commercial and industrial buildings as high as 65 per cent. In most other cases, including country real estate, they will lend no more than 50 to 55 per cent of valuation. Other assets that can be used for security include collectible debts, stock (of which they take the low value), and life policies with cash surrender values. Security to be offered must be clearly documented and listed. If it is property, provide the bank with all the necessary information, such as the volume and folio numbers, the address, even the current valuation (although they will still do their own).

A major part of romancing the bankers is to keep in touch. Don't just walk away after you have got your overdraft, or your loan, or your money invested. Keep in touch on a regular basis — at least every three to four months, more frequently if your business is going through a sticky patch or rapid growth. Maintain a close eye all day every day on your cash projections, amendments, and so forth. If there is a need for an extra overdraft or extra money for the business or things are going to get tight, talk to your bank manager in advance, provide him or her with cashflows and projections so that you can both predict what your needs will be. How much better it would be if a file note in the bank's file were to read: 'Mrs X telephoned to warn me of a cheque that she had drawn which might take her $1000 over the agreed limit. I told her this would be in order' rather than 'I had to telephone Mrs X to tell her the account was $1000 over the limit. I warned her that I might not pay the cheque next time.'

CASE STUDY:

Rosemary was in the convention business. She had worked for a number of companies before going into her own business with her eyes wide open about human follies and weaknesses. However, she struck cashflow problems. Rosemary had a good accountant, whom she had taken time to select. She worked strictly to the business plan prepared for her and always stayed in touch with her accountant and her banker, informing them of all developments in her business. Over the years she had socialised with the bank manager and established trust, she had honoured all her commitments, she made payments on all her borrowings when they were due, if not before. She had a good credit history. When the time came for her to take on a major new project, she had to consider a rapid expansion of staff and computer facilities. And when she asked for the money to do this, the bankers couldn't refuse.

Remember that a great deal of emphasis is placed on the integrity and management ability of the proprietors of any business. This can tip the scales in a marginal application for finance or investment. It is logical that the larger the amount of money required, the more professional your submission must be. You should familiarise yourself with the different types of loans, such as overdrafts, fully drawn advances or bill facilities. You should know what term of loan you want and what your business can afford. If it is a strong cash generator you can afford a reduction on the loan and payment of interest on an overdraft within a relatively short period of time. However, the term of the loan should be compatible with the cashflow forecast of the business. Quite often it is advisable to organise an interest-only loan, say for the first two years, before principal repayments are made if this is what matches the cashflow.

Deal with the negatives. If you ignore them in your plan, readers will wonder whether you are telling the whole story. Be aware of the flaws and weaknesses of your plan and be armed to address them clearly and concisely. Also anticipate any other negatives that the lender might raise. He or she might query your business's ability to meet its sales targets, especially in a poor economic environment. You will need to prove that these conditions have been taken into account and that the figures have been conservatively calculated.

To recap, the main things that lenders and investors look for is track record, cashflow and security. The relative importance of those three will vary. In hard times security tends to receive priority, then cashflow, then track record, but all three must stack up if you are to secure any money from the bank or an investor. Other criteria for the lender are likely to include:

- How much equity is the proprietor putting forward?
- What form or amount of security is being offered? What proportion does this represent of the total funds required?
- What is the income-generating ability of the activity? In other words, what is its viability?
- Is the market healthy/growing? Are changes expected in the market trend? The lender will often inspect the proposed site for the business and the situation of competition in the area.
- What is the character/integrity of the applicant? What previous track record does he or she have in the field? Heavy weight is given by loan officers and managers to an impression of integrity and genuineness.
- Does the applicant appear over-enthusiastic and under-researched? Is there an appropriate attitude of commitment, ideally demonstrated by a high equity contribution?
- What are the applicant's prior industry records?
- How much is required? Is it sufficient or excessive?
- What is the business classification? Is it capital intensive, involving purchase of plant and equipment and requiring long-term finance — for example, manufacturing, industry, transport, garages? Or is it labour intensive, involving high establishment costs, rental, stock and wages and predominantly short-term finance, for example, video hire outlets?
- What is the present state of technology? Will the equipment become obsolete? Also, what is the state of industrial relations within the industry?
- Is the business a new venture, not taking on any established concern? If so, all criteria will need to be scrutinised more closely.
- Will the business be a private company? If so, will the directors sign guarantees?
- What is the nature of the product or service? What role do seasonal factors play?

- Is the applicant impressive? Is the application well thought out? Obviously bank managers and loan officers have a good nose for quality in this regard.
- In the opinion of small business associations, how viable is the proposal?
- What are the applicant's credit ratings, value of accounts and connections?
- What is the standard of the accounting information given? Audited accounts are especially welcome even if statements contain a disclaimer.

Finally, and incidentally, the bank manager or investor will be interested to learn of any peripheral advantages to be derived from approving your loan or accepting your investment. For example, should any members of your family bank elsewhere, or perhaps at a different branch of the same bank, their business might be transferable. Look for other business to give the bank manager, such as foreign exchange operations, and so forth.

CREATIVE MONEY RAISING

Enterprisers in need of money tend to think automatically of borrowing. But external finance can also be obtained in the form of good old creditors. Most creditors allow at least one month's credit for purchases. So it is usually possible to rely on accommodation from this source to the amount of your material and other purchases. However, the amount owing to creditors tends to fluctuate during the month, and from month to month, due to the variation in the level of purchases. You will therefore need to allow for these fluctuations. You will have to build up a good reputation with the creditor before he or she will let you extend your terms. You would be most unwise to extend payments beyond the arrangement made, as this practice leads to loss of goodwill and loss of profit from failure to benefit from discounts. If you are going to use creditors and need extended time for payment, make sure you communicate in advance. Customers/debtors should also not be overlooked as a source of debt capital. If your product or service is important to them they may be willing to fund your business expansion by prepaying for your goods or services, or at least paying cash or paying earlier to help you through your rough patch.

Finance companies are a further source of external finance. They provide commercial construction and consumer loans for purposes such as purchase of equipment, leasing of plant or motor vehicles, working capital or even hire purchase. They also finance debt factoring as well as other loan facilities.

The sale of book debts, or factoring, can assist your company through difficult times. For some businesses factoring may be the only source of finance available, while for others it may be a stepping stone to a more sophisticated management, or (more likely) failure. Factoring tends to be extremely expensive and very hard to unwind. Only once have I seen a business come out of factoring better off.

Leasing plant and equipment is widely used as a means of obtaining capital resources for a business. The usual method is that the lessor purchases the plant from a supplier and then leases it to you for an agreed period. Of course, the real advantage of leasing is to conserve your capital. But it can be extremely expensive and you don't own the property. Don't do it just because it is tax deductible, because it still has a large cashflow effect. Also, in purchasing capital equipment of any kind it is always advisable to negotiate for trade-in allowances on old equipment, assuming this is appropriate. As an accountant and a lecturer in small business I am often asked what is the best way for a business to finance a car. There is usually a preconception that leasing is best, but this has come from motor car salespeople motivated by commissions on finance brokerage and the deduction of interest payable on the cars that are on the lot. Leasing is also often marketed as providing the best tax deduction, and taxation is certainly an important consideration but it should be the last. Leasing isn't always the best arrangement, especially if you can't afford it in the first place. You might be better off buying a second-hand car rather than leasing a new car. Remember the golden rule: self and family first, cashflow second, tax deduction last.

Another way to enhance your cashflow is to reorganise your

business and derive funds from the sale of any superfluous assets that are not earning adequate returns, such as surplus stock. This money can then be injected into more rewarding parts of the business to make profits.

If you have a heavy commitment to expand your business or to replace existing assets then you should retain a high percentage of your business profits for these purposes. If, on the other hand, you are not expanding or replacing existing assets there will still be the need for funds from retained profits. Remember, you need to finance not only real expansion but also expansion due to inflation.

Look at the possibility of putting your idle funds to work by cash budgeting and by eliminating the amounts kept for immediate needs. The essence of effective cash management is to keep idle dollars at an absolute minimum and any surplus working for you, earning interest.

Another way to free up funds is to keep tight credit control — keep your debtors to a minimum. (The importance of collecting promptly from your debtors is dealt with in detail in chapter 5.) Any stock you have on hand, including stationery, should be closely looked at. Do you need that much stock? Can buying be postponed till after the end of the month? Delaying purchases for a few days may give you an extra thirty days to pay. Stock is unsold sales. You would do better buying little and often rather than lots and seldom.

CASE STUDY:

Some enterprisers even generate cash by taking on a second job. I know a fellow who has a furniture factory. He had about twelve staff and, during a rough patch, he planned to do the work of three people to keep paying the others. I advised him to go back to his trade as an electrician and cut back his staff to a minimum. That is what he did and he is now back on track.

An alternative form of finance is the sale and lease-back of existing properties. This procedure enables the owner of a freehold property to sell the property to a finance institution, such as a life insurance company, then take a long lease on that property. The owner thereby realises the value of the property in hard cash and can use the funds to run the business. Sometimes an agreement to repurchase the property at the end of the lease period can be arranged.

Credit cards are another form of short-term finance for small businesses. Most financial institutions provide credit cards, such as Bankcard. They are convenient but expensive, with interest on cash advances being charged from the date of withdrawal and payable within fourteen days.

Often we hear talk about overseas money, with interest rates of five to ten per cent making a very attractive comparison with those on home ground. However, when the Australian dollar is at high levels, overseas borrowing presents some risks. Over and above the interest charges, a loan will cost a lot more to repay if the exchange rate fluctuates downwards during its term. You can protect yourself from this by taking out insurance called hedging. However, a true hedge will really only bring the two interest rates into line and will involve a further cost.

You should shop around when you are thinking of financing. Consider all the alternatives, including hire purchase (which is like leasing, except that you, not the finance company, own the goods). Weigh up the costs, the terms, the security required, and the appropriateness for your business. You will be amazed how much interest rates will differ, with, for example, people in the country paying up to two per cent more than those in the city.

It is also advisable during good times to line up sources of finance which you may not use, or to borrow even though you don't need to, just for the sake of establishing a credit rating. As we all know, it is very difficult to borrow money when times are tough but a good track record certainly helps.

In summary, you should keep the following factors in mind when seeking money:

- The best means of funding is maximising the use of money from within the business itself.

- Control expenses. Improve stock turnover. Make every effort to become and stay liquid and check the gross profit ratio. Many cash problems are only the evidence of other problems within the business.
- If you decide that you really do need outside funds, carefully budget all requirements to make sure you use the most satisfactory source of funds.
- Always remember that the state of the money market really determines how best to obtain your requirements.
- Usually short-term finance will meet short-term needs. Bridging finance, overdraft, bills of exchange, whether from banks or similar institutions, are a satisfactory way of solving your short-term needs, such as those caused by seasonal fluctuations, stock build-ups, major works in progress or needs for working capital.
- At all times preserve a borrowing potential for your business. In the end you will be bound by the resources that you can command and your ability to service them.
- When you are looking to raise finance externally you should shop around.
- Finally, always have available more than one source of finance — more than one bank, more than one finance company.

PART TWO:
BEING THERE

CHAPTER 5

Ingredients for Success

Important factors in ensuring the success of your small business, some of which have already been mentioned in this book, are as follows:

- Lead from the front, lead by example.
- Don't fool yourself. (Who are you trying to impress and why?) Don't let your ego take over.
- Plan long term. Be in for the marathon, not the sprint.
- Employ and associate only with the best people, especially those in management and administration. Make sure your staff are more intelligent or better qualified than you. Recognise that they are an asset to the business and pay them accordingly.
- Have more-than-adequate capital backing.
- Formulate monthly profit and loss balance figures. Compare with budget. Critically analyse cashflows. Always watch the bottom line — the profit line.
- Avoid the scourge of internal politics. Insecure non-achievers, in particular, love playing games, but these are destructive.
- Don't trust anyone without concrete reasons for doing so.
- Service your clientele. The client comes first, last and in between.

- Constantly listen, study and learn.
- Avoid the legal minefield.
- Commit early to quality, start with the best or what you think is going to be the best.
- Don't do things by half, don't accept second best.
- Dot your 'i's, cross your 't's. Do things properly the first time.
- Don't grow too quickly.
- Concentrate on cashflow. Ensure that it is always constant and sufficient to maintain the fuel you burn as your small business engine goes along. Make sure you have enough cash to start off with, that you don't go in having to borrow a lot of money. Always be tight, always be conservative.
- Make sure you build your business.
- Make sure you diversify in all senses — in terms of income sources, suppliers, staff, borrowing sources and investment.
- Look after your suppliers; pay them on time and make them your allies and your friends.
- Ensure that all your products and services are of the highest quality. Let them be your best advertisement.
- Constantly watch your overheads, particularly in a hard economic environment. Don't let a little bit of cashflow and profit get to you. Don't suddenly go out and have that overseas holiday or attend an expensive theatre or restaurant or buy that expensive car.
- Be organised, plan, keep track with good book-keeping and good housekeeping, have accurate information on how your business is performing.
- Don't fall into the habit of 'lazy marketing' — advertising in the newspapers, or going to a trade show, having a few drinks behind the counter and exhibiting your products. Get out there in the marketplace, wear the shoes out, knock on doors, make phone calls, keep going till it hurts. Get

bored, because when you are getting bored you are usually getting cashflow and, it is hoped, profits.

- Don't be too soft. Many businesses have been exploited because they were too nice. Know when to say 'No'. It is the most difficult word. Don't be swayed by people trying to sell you stock lines, things at a discount. Remember that stock is cash and you need that cash for your business.

- Manage your time efficiently, bearing in mind that you are probably the main, if not the only, income producer in your business.

CASE STUDY:

Four men, Barry, Paul, Gavin and Mark, combined to take over a retail wine and wholesale bottling business. Each of them was an expert in his own field. Barry was marketing manager of a timber production and distribution business, of which he was also a shareholder. Paul was a wine connoisseur and journalist. Gavin was a successful accountant and Mark was an expert marketing and public relations consultant.

When they took the business over it had not been very successful. It had cashflow and profit problems. One would think that the combination of these four experts would turn the business around or at least maintain it at its existing position of break-even to a small profit. Not so.

None of the four gave the venture the attention it deserved. Each took a part-time attitude, concentrating on his own business affairs to the detriment of the joint venture. Granted, they had lots of meetings and made lots of plans and, granted, their intentions were noble; but they did not manage to achieve anywhere near the prosperity that was possible. Within two years the business had been sold at a loss and, worse, all the partners had fallen out with each other.

SELL, PROFIT, COLLECT

Successful management of a business is a complex process which is dealt with in detail in chapter 6. However, of supreme importance, and therefore worth dealing with in advance, is the principle which lies at the heart of all successful commercial enterprise: sell, profit and collect.

If you don't *sell* your product or service, nothing else will happen. You can have the best accounting systems, the best products, the best staff, the best location; yet unless a sale is made, unless a deal is closed, you won't have any cashflow and you won't be able to pay your bills. However, despite its importance, don't get carried away with the sale as an end in itself. It's not the end; it's only the beginning.

Every service provided, every sale made, must be at a *profit*, otherwise the exercise is pointless. Because of its association with the excesses of big business, *profit* has become a dirty word. But in fact, restored to its original meaning, it is merely a healthy measure of the effectiveness of management in satisfying the wants of the consumer. It is no coincidence that many of the firms that make good profits also offer the customer best value for money.

Knowing what your costs are, knowing that you will make a profit, takes the anxiety and worry out of your business. You should know exactly (per day, per week, per month) what sales you need to make in order to cover all your costs — in other words, what your break-even point is. As an employee of your own business, you should include in your costs what you would be paid in another business, then add a profit margin for the risk and the return on your money invested. Add up your overheads — rent, wages (yours and your staff's) — interest on money borrowed, dividends to anyone who has invested in your business, stock and purchases, and sell at an amount above that to make a profit. Then you can reinvest in the business, you can grow to the level that you want in accordance with your business plan.

As we saw in chapter 3, one of the biggest mistakes most

people make when they first start off in business is that they feel compelled to undercut their competitors. But pricing is a matter of confidence — in your product, in your service and in yourself. Most businesses offer a service or product which rests on years or decades of experience, and this experience should be costed into the price. (This reminds me of a story I once heard about Picasso in a restaurant: A woman asked the great man to scribble something on a napkin, saying she would be happy to pay whatever he felt it was worth. Picasso obliged and said, 'That will be $10,000.' The astonished woman replied, 'But you did that in thirty seconds.' 'No,' Picasso said, 'it took me forty years to do that.')

And finally, having sold at the appropriate profit, you must *collect* your money. There is no point in a sale or provision for profit unless you get paid. Perhaps it should be the first consideration in these hard times — don't make sales to customers who cannot assure you of payment. Money owed to your business is effectively a type of unsecured loan. If you, in turn, have borrowed money from the bank to finance your business, it is costing you interest not to collect what is owed to you. When money is in short supply, as it is now, it is more important than ever before that you run a tight ship in collecting from your debtors and repaying your creditors, otherwise the banks could close down your business by deciding to call in your overdraft facility or other loans.

Debtors lists should be kept up to date and arranged in order of size of debt. Imagine the impact if your largest debtor announced its liquidation to you tomorrow. Apart from the profit content of the debt, what would be the out-of-pocket loss to your business? Would you be able to sustain such a loss? Study the spread of your risks. Do you have a large number of small debtors or perhaps a heavy reliance on a hard core or just a few? Examine the aging of your debtors ledger. A well-maintained debtor system will give you a monthly report of debtors split between current, 30, 60 and 90 days and over. What percentage of your total debtors is in each category, in both number and dollar value?

You must also examine the policies you use as a basis for giving credit. If the profit margin is low then the out-of-pocket loss in bad debts will be high, so there is every justification for keeping the terms very tight. (They should always be tight anyway!) Examine the steps you use to assess new accounts. Information to be sought will include account name and address, whether it is a company, partnership or sole trader or trust, reference from a bank or another supplier, years in business, names and addresses of directors and credit limit requested. Don't be lazy in this area. Do your homework and make sure you check out the potential customer thoroughly. Visit any larger potential customers worth considering. This can help you gain an insight into the business. Points to consider would include the morale of the business, appraisal of the proprietor, level of business activity, office system, quality of equipment and so on. Sales personnel are generally less inclined to be critical in their evaluation of new and existing clients, for obvious reasons. Hence the need for an independent review.

In some industries it is possible to reduce the risk of extending credit by obtaining directors' guarantees to company accounts, a cash price with an order or upon delivery of goods, your retention of title to goods after delivery or until payment is made, trade credit insurances, reciprocal dealings providing ability to set off between accounts, or, in some cases, the taking of security such as a bank guarantee or a charge over an asset of the customer. Most of these will not be available on a normal trade account, but if the stakes are high then you should adopt all or some of these securities. It should always be remembered that the extension of credit carries with it the need for providing additional cash, the cost of which is interest, whether paid or foregone (this is called the opportunity cost).

Dealing with slow payers should be planned well in advance and should follow a set procedure. It may involve the issuing of an 'account rendered' statement followed by demands for payment, reference to a credit agency or a solicitor, or simply presenting in person. Amongst small business customers those responsible are usually the owners, who should be easy to identify and locate. Be positive in your collection effort and remember what we have already mentioned about friendship: be friends with your customers and they are more likely to pay you promptly.

Your operation's literature and invoices must make very clear your payment terms — 7, 14, 30 or 60 days. In the past, 60 days was the normal trading term, but nowadays you should insist on payment at least within 30 days. If your debtors haven't paid by the due date they should be closely monitored, probably weekly, and followed up with statements, reminder letters and telephone calls.

When attempting to collect an overdue account obtain a specific and personal promise for payment. Write in your diary the promise and the name of the person who made it. Not only will this procedure allow you to keep track and collect more easily, it will give you more confidence in approaching the debtor when following up on a broken promise. Do not believe anyone in an Accounts Payable department who tells you that the payments are computer controlled and that the process cannot be interrupted or circumvented. Any company, large or small, has the capability to hand-write cheques.

Cash discounts can be used effectively. By giving discounts, where applicable, to prompt payers you are rewarding your reliable customers and encouraging them to continue trading with you. This is a positive approach and eliminates bad feelings. You should first calculate the cost of this discount to your business and show the applicable rates in the official price list given to every eligible customer.

In hard times there is no point in being soft with slow payers. If someone owes your business money and your reminders fall on deaf ears, just go and sit in their office until you get a result. If embarrassment doesn't work, then go right in with the legals. Issue a Section 364, which is a company wind-up, or a Notice of Bankruptcy for individuals. Get in and get your money, and always bank it on the date of receipt.

You might also consider selling on credit cards such as Bankcard, American Express, and so on. At least you will be guaranteed payment by a fixed time after the sale, but make sure you build their charges into your costs. Another way to ensure payment is to take security over your customers in the form of personal guarantees. Most importantly, supply only customers who have a proven capacity to pay. Do a credit check — have the customer fill in all the necessary information, then ring up and verify it. Don't rely on bank opinion; it's not enough.

Very few businesses do not have some bad debt. Intending customers seeking credit should offer trade and bank references which should always be checked thoroughly. Enquiries should be made with local employee groups. Bank credit checks are invariably vague, but if you have a close relationship with your own bank manager he or she will probably be able to interpret and expand on them for you.

CASE STUDY:

I met Evan some ten years ago. His father had spent thirty years building up his own electrical business in Sydney. Business had flourished, even though Evan's father did not have sophisticated reporting systems. The reasons were basic: he had a grip on all his costs, he never borrowed money and he had loyalty from his employees, serviced his customers and collected his money.

On the last day of each month Evan's father would work into the wee hours and then drive to the post office to mail out the invoices for prompt payment. Eventually Evan took over the running of the business. But he didn't have quite the same attitude to cash. He was more interested in electricals than in management. Evan also had enormous family troubles which he anguished over and which distracted him from the business. He then started to drink excessively. He didn't dot the 'i's and cross the 't's, and he didn't pay attention to cashflow.

His business has recently collapsed. He couldn't even sell it, so excessive were the liabilities. For all his efforts and generosity in handing over a business worth $3m net, Evan's father is barely going to have enough money to retire on. The lessons here are many.

A perfectly good business could come unstuck due to the failure of its major clients. It could also have a preference claim brought against it. If a debtor who is in difficulty pays you and then goes into liquidation or becomes bankrupt the administrator can come back at you and claw back the money if it is considered to be a preferential payment. One way to protect yourself against those types of situations is to know your customers. Another way, if you have particularly large customers or large sales, is to try to get a letter of credit, that is, a document guaranteeing that the customer's bank will pay you on set terms and conditions — say, when goods are supplied or when they are dispatched. A letter of credit is more commonly used in overseas transactions. Probably more widely known is the bank guarantee. As we have already noted, small business people are quite often required to give their bankers a personal guarantee. Why not get a bank guarantee from your customers to ensure that they will pay you? Subscribe to the trade journals — for example, *College Gazette* — to keep an eye on bad debtors. Watch the economy and think about the industry you are in and the industries that your customers are in, and whether there are any adverse economic conditions that might affect their ability to pay.

Another form of protection against non-payment is trade indemnity insurance, whereby you pay a fee to have your insurance company pay up if your customer doesn't pay. Legal action might be considered as a last resort, but weigh up the costs involved, and remember that there is still no guarantee that you will get paid.

A trusting relationship with your customer is probably the most efficient way of guaranteeing payment. Should they get into a bit of financial bother they're sure to pay you first if you are a friend, the one who sees them socially.

BUILDING GOOD RELATIONSHIPS

In the context of increasingly impersonal business practice, you are more likely to receive quality attention and therefore to be successful (and not only in the area of debt collection) if you can build amicable and trusting relationships with the key players in your particular field.

Most people realise the importance of getting on well with their customers. But don't forget your suppliers. If you have always paid your creditors on time, then they will allow you extra credit should the need arise, and this might be particularly valuable in tough times. Don't abuse your creditors. The minute you abuse them they will try to wind you up, liquidate you. Develop a good rapport with them, be honest with them and be trustworthy. Get close to them. Perhaps take them to the theatre or to something else of mutual interest. Treat your creditors fairly and warmly, then, should things go badly for you, they will treat you fairly and warmly in return. They will think of you in personal, rather than statistical, terms.

The same applies to your bank manager. The biggest problem for bank managers is that small business people don't talk to them enough. Don't hide from your bank manager; face up to him/her and the issues that concern him/her, provide him/her with a business plan (see chapter 3). Update him/her with financial statements every month, every six months or every twelve months. Tell him/her of your cashflow requirements. Attend to your budget and liquidity problems. Let him/her know in advance if you need any extra money or, indeed, if you have any extra money to invest. Talk to him/her, get close to him/her. Get his/her advice. He/she is very experienced, he/she has a lot of small businesses amongst his/her clients and might well pass on valuable information to you. When you need that extra overdraft or extra credit facility he/she will allow you to have it, provided he/she knows you will pay it out.

Don't make promises you can't keep. There's nothing worse for a lender or a creditor. If you say you will pay by the fourteenth of the following month, make sure you do pay by that date, if not earlier. Don't keep making excuses. If you make a commitment be sure to stick to it. Bear in mind that bankers are highly trained and highly audited. Their files are detailed. They are avid writers, they record every conversation, they keep very detailed file notes. You should do the same: make notes, record your conversations with the bank, and you will be in a better position to stand by the agreed arrangements.

Your accountant, like your bank manager, should be someone you talk to constantly. Develop a friendship, get free advice, invite him/her home to dinner, let him/her contribute to your business plan. Get him/her involved in your business, but not too closely (accountants have to remain impartial and professional so as not to lose their independence).

So, underlying your relationships with your accountant, your bank manager and your creditors is the need for communication, honesty and trust. These are as important to business as the other factors we have mentioned. Everyone wants to deal with someone who is honest and trustworthy because there are so many shonks out there. If you are honest and upright, you may offer a service or product which costs more, and you may not be able to deliver it as quickly as someone else, but because you are a friend, because you are trusted and liked, you will clinch the deal, you will get the order. Suppliers will supply you before they supply someone else because they want you to be successful. Your customers will pay you on time. The bank manager will give you that extra advice. The accountant will return your call, will give you those extra few minutes, that extra bit of devoted energy that is necessary to help your business survive and achieve its profit and goals.

CHAPTER 6

Managing a Small Business

Managing a small business is very similar to managing your personal affairs. Basically, you must make sure you budget properly and make sure more money comes in than goes out. There are perhaps a few more complications when it comes to business, but generally people who can manage their own personal finances tend to be able to manage their business finances as well. The following pages offer detailed suggestions for the effective management of a small business.

GETTING GOOD ADVICE

Many small business operators make the mistake of trying to do everything themselves. Not one of them would contemplate doing their own mail deliveries, yet they don't consult the experts in the truly specialised areas.

For general advice, especially on finance, government small business agencies can be very helpful. In addition, build around you a team of useful advisers, each with their own field of expertise. Choose them carefully and don't base your decision on convenience, friendship or family. The various associations and institutes will give you lists of members in your locality. Don't rush into a quick decision. Shop around, talk to a few people, have a few meetings. Find advisers who show empathy and care, can be trusted, are prepared to understand the needs of your business and are experienced. Don't be afraid of changing later if you are dissatisfied, just as you would if you were dissatisfied with your doctor. Good advisers bring objectivity to your business, possibly recognising early warning signs that you might have missed because you are too involved, and seeing problems for what they really are. They will put you back in touch with the wider economic context at the times when a fresh and ruthless perspective matters most.

Let's look at the different advisers a small business needs. The first is the *accountant.* A good accountant can provide advice and assistance in all aspects of financial management, sources of finance and applying for finance. It is a mistake to use accountants only to prepare annual accounts and taxation returns. Their expertise extends much more widely than this and it pays to tap it. You should choose your accountant in the early stages of your business, when you are developing your plan, and periodically review his or her ability to service your business needs.

Make sure your accountant is strong and commands your respect. There's no point paying for advice and not taking it, which occurs too often. A good accountant can help an average business to succeed, but an average accountant can help a good business to fail. Deal with accountants who are successful themselves. If they can't manage their own affairs, how are they going to manage yours? Interview at least three candidates. Find out about their services and charges, and how they operate.

Choose an accountant who knows your industry and business area, someone who can readily determine from your monthly figures any potential financial problems or, indeed, any potential opportunities. He or she will understand your business plan and your costings and everything else that is peculiar to your business area. He or she knows who the lenders are, who the bad customers are. Good accountants are specialists just like other professionals. It's no good going to one who specialises in hotels if you are running a farm, as each of these types of business requires vastly different knowledge and experience.

Talk to your industry peers. Ask them who they use, who they are satisfied with, who does the best job for them. Don't be afraid to use the same accountant.

You must feel comfortable with your accountant. It is no good going to an accountant who hasn't got time for you and doesn't answer your phone calls. Once you have found a suitable accountant, don't assume that the level of service is guaranteed. Rarely does the accountant who originally suited your business continue to do so throughout all its phases. The probability is that you will outgrow your accountant or your accountant will outgrow you. But, as we said earlier, a good personal rapport can help stem this process and hold your accountant's interest. If you get along well, you are less likely to be overlooked when your accountant is under pressure.

Most small business people start off with either production or sales skills and generally lack financial management skills. Therefore, the accountant is probably the most important adviser and is central to the business's financial management. So stay close to her/him, keep her/him involved and informed. Take her/him to the first meeting with the bank manager. Consider inviting your accountant to your monthly or fortnightly meetings. Make sure you send the agenda for perusal in advance so that every second spent in the meeting is fully productive. Watch your accountant's charge-out rates. Make sure you get quotes in advance. Watch out for those accountants who charge you for the lunches they take you to. (It's a good way for them to make money while they're being fed.) In hard times, when your business may not be travelling too well, the choice of an expert accountant to come in and review your affairs might mean the difference between surviving and collapsing.

Another important adviser is your *bank manager*. You should talk to your bank manager when your business venture is merely a glint in your eye. Tell him/her you are tossing around ideas and would welcome his/her opinion, even though you may not yet have identified your financing needs. A good relationship with your bank manager is important as his/her experience enables him to provide worthwhile advice. If the bank is unable to accommodate your financial requirements your bank manager can probably suggest the best alternative. Remember, banks deal with small businesses every day of the week. Among their many clients are those who have been around for a long time and have extensive experience. During the early stages of developing your business plan your bank manager can often help by pointing out the pitfalls. Banks see the good and the bad sides of business, they know what it is like for families to be kicked out of their home, they know what it is like to repossess. It is in their interests to try to help you not to become a bankruptcy statistic.

Yet another important adviser is the *solicitor*. Proper legal advice in business may save you thousands of dollars and even a spell in gaol. But seeking advice in a hurry may land you in trouble, so it is a good idea to start looking for a suitable solicitor before you need one.

The law is a very complex animal and legal practices tend to specialise in particular aspects of the law — for example, tax, contracts, tenancy, product liability, employee legislation and litigation, conveyancing, and so on. Make sure you find one who suits your needs in each particular situation (this means you may end up using several, on different occasions). Whether to use a large or a small firm very much depends on the size of your business. Initially I would suggest you start off with a smaller firm, the bigger ones tending to be far too expensive and appropriate only for specialist advice.

Get referrals from friends and advice from your employer association as to who is the best in a particular area. Indeed, there are lawyers who specialise in different industries. Try out one or two and make sure you strike the right relationship of trust, empathy, care and professionalism. Legal fees can cost a fortune, therefore you must at least make sure you get quotations before you engage the services of a lawyer.

Any legal agreement your business has or is considering undertaking should be examined by your solicitor to ensure your best interests are being protected. It makes sense to seek his or her advice on options open to you before decisions are made.

CASE STUDY:

Julia inherited a great deal of money due to the tragically premature death of her husband. At the age of thirty-two she had a house worth $320,000 without any borrowings, a $1m life insurance pay-out and a marketing/public relations/advertising firm about which she knew nothing. She had shared with her husband the responsibility of looking after their three children, aged 2, 6 and 10. What was Julia to do now?

Through her husband she had met a man who had been in the same business but was now retired. She knew he wouldn't be competing with, or trying to destroy, her business, so she trusted him. He urged her to get good advisers and after much research she ended up with a number of accountants and lawyers to choose from. She asked all the accountants who their existing clients were, where their money was invested, what business interests they had that might conflict with hers, how many employees they had, how much time they had available, how their health was and whether or not they would be accessible to her. All three accountants sounded impressive, but only one took the time to present a detailed analysis of Julia's personal and business financial position. He got a new client.

As for the lawyer, that choice was slightly more difficult. Eventually Julia chose one who had the toughness needed to compensate for her lack of confidence, who knew her way around the industry and was able to advise Julia on the legal aspect of continuing with the business.

The children are not seeing as much of their mum as they once did, but the business certainly continues to prosper.

Insurance is of critical importance to small business, as will be seen later. All lending institutions will insist that applicants for finance have sufficient insurance to replace stock, plant and buildings and to cover loss of profits. *Insurance brokers* should therefore be included on your team of advisers. Remember that in life generally you only get what you pay for and the cheapest may thus not be the best for you. Your broker will tell you what should be covered and by whom. He or she will get several quotes and is equipped to choose the most suitable package.

Another form of advice can be sought from *management consultants,* who usually specialise in a particular area, such as sales, marketing, finance or production. Be very wary of management consultants. Work only with those who have proved to be successful in the past. Many are spent forces and the only reason they consult is because they lack practical expertise themselves. Make sure you get quotes from management consultants, and, indeed, any other consultants you engage, so that you know exactly what to expect.

From time to time it is a good idea to get a *sales professional* to come in and provide some inspirational sparks to enhance the performance of your staff. They can often set new standards and working styles. But make sure you tailor their input to your needs. Don't give them vague instructions — give them specific tasks, otherwise you won't get anywhere.

Stockbrokers and *merchant banks* should also be mentioned, although they confine their advisory services almost exclusively to large companies. In special circumstances they may assist small businesses. For example, if a company has a sound and profitable venture in mind but few resources, a merchant banker may be able to link up the company with potential investors. Alternatively, the bank may involve itself directly. Merchant banks are generally willing to take comparatively high risks if the potential rewards are also high. In addition, both stockbrokers and merchant bankers provide special advice and assistance on mergers and takeovers and again the latter may be willing to provide financial assistance.

And finally, when selecting your advisers, don't overlook a *mentor* and/or an *external director*. In past societies the mentor relationship was commonly that between grandfather and grandson, who lived in the same town or even the same house. The carpenter passed on his skills in carpentry, the builder his building skills, the banker his banking skills, and so on. That social structure is now lost forever, but the benefits of the general principle still apply. A mentor, by definition, should be much more experienced, wiser and probably therefore older than you. Ideally he or she should have business expertise in the area in which you work, but a background in banking or finance would also be valuable. Listen to everything your mentor has to say and take his or her advice; at first it might make little sense, but in the long run you will be the better for having heard it.

A strong, experienced external director, like the mentor, can be invaluable to the growing business. Choose someone you trust and respect and will take notice of, to keep you in check and to guide, console and encourage you when things are tough.

NETWORKING

The exchange of useful information by people in a particular industry is known as networking. Networking vehicles can be formal, such as those provided by employer groups, clubs, societies and courses; or informal, such as those that spring up socially, for example at the local gymnasium. Whatever their context they are potentially very powerful in establishing and raising standards and in introducing participants to knowledge and opportunities.

Many self-employed business people are isolated by their need to work long hours and concentrate on the task at hand. This makes some form of organised interaction with industry peers even more important. You should take every opportunity to meet with other small business owners, talk to them and listen to them. Much of the knowledge that contributes to running a prosperous business cannot be gained through formal training — it is gleaned through experience and is passed on by sharing that experience. You will find that your peers also have cashflow problems, staff problems and finance problems. They are probably going through the same thing as you. Listen to how they solve their problems, discuss your solutions with them. By talking to others in the same boat you can share ideas and concerns, be comforted and help each other. It might be a good idea to organise a monthly breakfast with a group of like-minded business people.

THE EXTERNAL ENVIRONMENT

You cannot afford to ignore the external economic environment in the running of your business, in fact you should cut your cloth according to how you think the economy is going to pan out. You need only scan the business section of the newspapers and business magazines to realise the extent to which our personal lives, let alone our business lives, are affected by oil prices, interest rates, politics, even an apparently harmless statement by the Treasurer.

The size of the impact depends on the specific industry and market you are in. For example, a rise in petrol prices will have a greater impact on a transport company than on a company that develops computer software. A rise in interest rates will affect the demand for property and therefore decrease business prospects for real estate firms and property developers. Manufacturing businesses suffer massive repercussions when the Government pulls the plug on tariffs, as it did in the 1970s with respect to the clothing, footwear, tyre and carpet industries. At the moment the car industry is overstocked and huge numbers of workers have been laid off. This means that there is not going to be further development of new models for some time and, down the track, that will hurt the suppliers.

Increased demands on your work schedule in a tough economic climate are no excuse not to keep yourself informed. In fact, such a climate makes it all the more important for you to remain alert to the macro-economic environment — to watch for external guidance, warnings and opportunities. If you stick your head in the sand and focus only on the immediate problems of your own operation, you will lose sight of the big picture, the scene that really matters. Your business is only a cog in a big commercial machine — don't lose sight of its context. As I said at the outset, read, listen, watch and learn. Make sure you educate yourself in the meaning of terms such as *elasticity/*

inelasticity of prices, the J curve, inflation, recession, depression, balance of payments and *tariffs* (see Bibliography, page 240). Buy and borrow books, attend courses, go to your employer association meetings, be part of a network of business acquaintances.

Whenever you hear or see a piece of economic, political or even social or scientific news, always try to envisage how that fragment of information will affect your business, what impact it will have on your sales or your expenses or on your customers and your suppliers. For example, if you are a retailer in a suburban shopping centre and you learn by mail or by reading the local newspaper that there are going to be substantial improvement works in your street for the next four months, what do you do? You don't lash out and complain — ultimately the improvements will benefit your business. You find out the exact details. Attend local council meetings, speak to the council's engineering department, find out when the works are starting, what is involved, when they will be completed (add on two or three months to allow for delays). In anticipation of fewer customers, plan to reduce stock, to organise holidays for yourself and your staff, and to refurbish your shop if appropriate. In other words, minimise your costs, budget for a reduction in cashflow and take advantage of the opportunity. You will probably also need to pump up your marketing in order to warn customers beforehand and bring them back once the works are completed.

Familiarise yourself with trends and cycles, and take advantage of these in your business. You can even prosper from the hard economic environment itself. A Melbourne University economist, Dr Duncan Ironmonger, has observed that in a recession people do more work around the house. We cook a few more meals at home, we do more of our own car and house repairs because having less paid work gives us more time for unpaid work (for which we would normally have to pay someone else) and we re-plant the garden because we can't afford to go away on holidays. In such times, the products that sell well are staples such as food, renovating materials, paint, garden accessories, plants, and homewares such as pots and pans — but only for the domestic market, not for the trade. Also, people cut back on big things (such as cars) and splurge on little things (such as clothing accessories and cheap entertainment) to make themselves feel good. Service industries that do well are those that clean up the mess — financial advisers, insolvency accountants and lawyers, antique and art auctioneers.

CASE STUDY:

I read recently about an enterprising retailer who, right in the midst of the recession, opened up a gift shop with a fairy theme. 'There is nothing in the shop that anyone needs,' she was quoted as saying. 'I'm selling dreams, magic and good feelings.' At first she was scared to tell her accountant about her undertaking, but within weeks of opening she was taking on extra staff and had been approached by two people wanting to franchise the business. Such was the misjudged pessimism of her suppliers that the only difficulty she experienced was keeping up with demand.

By the same token, businesses that might flourish in a recession need to watch for other external factors that might affect them adversely. Plant nurseries, for example, would be wise to take conservative action in the face of climatic disasters, such as drought or floods. The insolvency accountancy firm would benefit in better times from also specialising in, say, tax planning.

Furthermore, no two recessions are exactly the same, and their causes partly determine their effects on business. In Australia's most recent recession, export industries have been less affected because the downturn has been due largely to domestic factors, such as high interest rates and the Federal Government's drive to curb demand. However, industries dependent on government contracts, such as computer software suppliers, have been hit badly in Victoria due to regional factors.

113

You need to understand how all these factors might affect you. In your time management allocate quality, concentrated time to absorb and analyse what is going on around you. Don't cling rigidly to pre-conceived ideas about your business or the context in which it operates. Be adaptable, be innovative. (Remember the proverb: Necessity is the mother of invention.) Think laterally, allow your instinct to guide you, listen to other points of view. In tough times, when your head is down and your tail is up just to keep your cashflow going, the assistance of your mentor or external director would be invaluable in this regard. Even though they may be under financial pressures themselves, they are still likely to bring a wider, independent perspective to your business.

BUSINESS HARDWARE

In your business plan you should list all the physical needs of your business, and decide what you can afford and when.

Your business premises are one of your most important tools of trade, and there are many variables to consider. Should you work from home or from an office? How much space do you need? Should you rent or purchase?

Make sure you locate well. Many small business industries fail to appreciate how costly bad positioning can be. Are you physically accessible to your customers? Are you in the ideal situation to receive and deliver goods to service them? What transport is available for your staff? What other facilities are available? Will the staff be happy there? Is it safe, is it secure? Is theft a problem? Is there a risk of fire? Will you be proud to welcome your customers and visitors? What is the best way to get raw materials in and products and services out? It's in your interests to ensure that your premises are safe; after all, accidents are costly.

If you are in retail, how large should the store be? What merchandise needs to be displayed? Can more stock be securely stored? Are existing displays and shelving adequate for merchandising needs? Are counters and tools well positioned? Are there sufficient points of sale? Does the store layout induce customers to buy more? Are stock control methods adequate?

Vehicles are also important business hardware, and again there are many options. Should you use your own vehicles, or should you use hired or rented vehicles or courier services? What type of vehicles do you need? Do you need the headache of initially running your own vehicle and driver? Should you hire purchase or lease? Talk to your accountant about this. As we have seen, the decision to lease is too often driven by the hope of a so-called tax advantage, which may be unfounded. Make sure whatever you use has a profit or net profit result or net cashflow gain first and a tax benefit last.

Be careful when buying second-hand equipment — it can often cause problems. Frustrating delays or additional footwork through lack of forethought can adversely affect your workers and profits. If your machinery is delicate, regular maintenance is essential. The more complex the plant, the more thought you should put into selecting and acquiring your equipment.

Keep abreast of the latest technology and the equipment being used by your competitors. Business might be lost overnight to someone else who can provide a more rapid turnover or higher quality article at the same unit cost. Be one step ahead of the factory inspector from the Department of Labour and Industry.

Computers, and their cost-saving advantages, must be considered.

Find out about, and adhere to, government standards affecting production layout, storage of raw materials and finished goods, work safety and comfort.

PEOPLE

It is no coincidence that labour costs eat up a large proportion of turnover in most businesses. Quality of staff really is the most important factor in any business of more than one person, therefore you should always employ the best people you can obtain and afford. Friendly, skilful, conscientious staff will enhance work pace by putting in the extra effort — without complaint. If your employees are satisfied and feel cared for

115

they will stay put, and stable personnel will mean a more efficient business.

One of the great satisfactions in running your own business comes from building a solid team of workers around you who support and carry out the policies and plans of the business. But harmonious working relationships, high morale and effective team work — features of the ideal staff — do not just happen; bear these features in mind when selecting staff and foster them in the on-going situation.

Each person on the staff has a responsibility to all other members to perform his or her task efficiently and cheerfully, to help others willingly when their work requires it, to accept the authority that goes with the job and to back up seniors loyally during the good and the bad times. In small businesses in particular, if there is just one person in the group who falls short in any of these respects the efficiency of the whole team is reduced, not only in terms of total output but also in terms of influence on other members of the group.

The business owner has a particularly important role to play in the group by virtue of his or her position. As the leader, he or she must ensure that all members of the group get maximum satisfaction from their work, enjoy happy relations with their fellows and work with enthusiasm and efficiency to achieve the objectives of the business.

When you are employing people make sure that there is a clear mutual understanding of the basis upon which they are being employed. If a new recruit is not a member of a union and is not being employed under an award, but just being employed generally, you should provide a letter of engagement which spells out the basis on which he or she is being employed, the pay, hours of work and duties, and what period of notice is required if either party wants to bring the situation to an end. This will save problems later on.

Staff should have clearly defined jobs and the employer must see that they do them well. They should be given adequate initial training and then be allowed to work with just enough supervision to ensure that they keep up to the required standard. Constant fussing and checking is likely to lower a person's pride. On the other hand, insufficient supervision allows errors to go uncorrected and makes workers feel that their superior is not interested in whether the work is done well or poorly. Each staff member should know what is expected of him/her in terms of the extent and the quality of their work. If they exceed expectations, they are entitled to, and should receive, fair praise for their achievements. Recognition of one's efforts is always pleasurable, particularly if it has been genuinely earned. Fatuous praise is worthless.

If a person falls short of the standard expected of them the wise employer does not just condemn without trial. Talk with the employee and try to find out the cause of the failure. The fault may be not with the person but in the work system — the tools, the conditions; or it may be due to lack of guidance at the outset or personal troubles at home. If you have been successful in building up a sound relationship of mutual confidence and respect the worker will be glad to get such troubles off his or her chest and ask for assistance in putting things right. Be constructive in your criticisms and when mistakes are discovered ensure that they are not repeated. Progress is not made without occasional errors, but you as the employer are failing somewhere if the same error occurs frequently.

You should encourage your staff to learn new work so that they are gradually being prepared for more responsibility and greater rewards. Dull, routine jobs will be more interesting if the person doing them not only understands the next step but is given some training towards doing it themselves. They also take a greater interest and more pride in their job if they are given some responsibility for training their successor.

It is important to keep your staff informed of your business objectives, so they can be motivated to the same extent to which you are, especially when the operation is small and growing. They must have the same or nearly the same amount of interest in, and understanding of, how the business succeeds — through selling, making a profit and collecting the money. (Your business plan will serve to demonstrate this to them.)

If you can make the objectives of the employee and the objectives of the company one and the same, you have a greater chance of succeeding at both.

Because you will often be unavailable, it is important to delegate authority and foster initiative, not forgetting that authority and responsibility go together. The ability to think for oneself and make decisions varies from person to person. The wise owner encourages staff to work out solutions to their own problems because decisions should be made as closely as possible to the level at which they are put into effect. Of course you should check each decision, but the staff involved should be encouraged to suggest their own solution first.

Make sure all employees are doing the jobs for which they are best suited and that they don't have some undiscovered talent. Watch out for signs that staff are outgrowing their jobs and promote them at the right time. It may be hard to lose the services of a good worker to another area but it is even harder to lose that worker altogether. More difficult to deal with are those who have come as far as their capabilities allow but think they should be promoted by virtue of long and competent service. The best course of action here is frankness. Ask them if they really think they are capable of taking on the higher position. If they are sensible and the position is clearly portrayed, they will probably admit that the work would be beyond them, and while they will be disappointed at least they will know where they stand.

It is important to try to make the workplace as comfortable, practical and enjoyable as possible but frivolity should not be encouraged at the expense of efficiency. Make sure you get on well with all your staff, without becoming too close, and show them that you care about them, because that is what really helps them to be motivated and profitable for you. Take an interest in their development. Care about their safety, health and general well-being. Treat people as people, not as numbers on a payroll. Make it your business to know about any major personal problems and provide constructive help without becoming too close. You should remain alert to any tension or unease in, or amongst, your staff. You should watch for any lack

118

of commitment or prevalence of a nine-to-five mentality, both of which denote staff discontent and undermine the prosperity of the business.

It is not always the big pay increase that will retain and protect your people. More effective are your appreciation and recognition of their efforts and achievements — give them a 'pat on the back' with flowers, tickets, gifts, lunches or dinners. In this country at the moment it is quite legal (albeit taxable, but at a rate lower than income tax) to provide benefits to employees — the second car for the family, school fees, holidays or something smaller. Fringe benefits need not cost a lot, but they may be just what is required to motivate your staff and retain them.

Of particular relevance in hard times is the skilful handling of grievances. Complaints should be examined clinically and without prejudice or blame to establish whether the underlying cause is a shortcoming of the worker or a problem with their environment, their relationship with others or the company's policies. Listen patiently with an open mind and distinguish facts from opinions. Get to the bottom of the real issue, check and consult. Be fair, be hard and be careful not to set negative precedents. You must at all times exercise self-control, as emotions can run high in such situations. Resolve the issue by consensus if possible but avoid unnecessary delays in reaching a decision. Discontent soon spreads and speedy rough justice without prejudice or rancour is far better than excessive deliberation over a decision. Explain your decision in a clear and straightforward manner and make sure you keep detailed records of all meetings and significant documents.

Every effort should also be made to ensure that the work situation is safe and healthy. Safety is everyone's responsibility. You must not only provide a safe environment but also ensure that employees take reasonable care. Adequate safety equipment should be supplied to each employee. Ensure that your business complies with relevant safety requirements. Safety training should be carried out at regular intervals and safety audits should be undertaken by you at set times. Officers from your State's Occupational Health and Safety Commission or the National Safety Council can assist in drawing up a safety policy and carrying out safety awareness programmes.

In tough times there is a lot of pressure on small business staff. Creditors phone frequently for payment, debtors aren't paying, there is stress and strain. More than ever, in this environment, there is a need for you to communicate and be honest with your staff. Communicate your plans, expectations, problems and opportunities. Carry out staff suggestions on ways to improve the organisation. Set realistic targets and constantly review their work. If you are in desperate straits you needn't reveal every last detail, but you should at least let your staff know what the general financial situation is. In hard times employees often start to worry about the viability of their employer, so it is far better to be honest about it than to have them inflate it and resign due to uncertainty.

When times are tough it is more critical than ever for you to confine yourself to quality human resources. So a short note on recruitment methods is warranted here. Recruitment is a process of obtaining personnel who meet the requirements of your business. Although recruitment is generally applied to obtaining applicants from outside the company many companies have an unrecognised source of applicants from within their own ranks. It goes without saying, therefore, that the possibility of transferring and promoting existing people should always be considered before taking on anyone from outside. Promotion from within can minimise the cost of training new people because the person concerned already has a knowledge of the company and its products. Familiarity with the company's procedures also makes adjustment to the new position easier.

Above all you should prepare a detailed job specification. Of course it might change with time, it might vary as times get tougher, but it should be regularly updated. The job specification should spell out the required job experience, skills or education and training, as well as any other relevant requirements such as age, physique, health, aptitude and temperament. Make sure that all information is as detailed and accurate as humanly possible. Too often applicants are sought to fill positions to which little thought has been given. As a result a wrong placement is made.

There are various ways of obtaining new staff from outside. Obviously you can advertise in the papers and you can go through staff recruitment agencies (these charge quite a substantial percentage of the first year's wages in fees). You can advertise in industry magazines — for example, accounting magazines if you are looking for an accountant. You can also ask your existing employees and friends whether they know of anyone who is suitable for the job. (Be careful with this approach, though, and don't neglect your usual criteria for suitability.) The Commonwealth Government has an employment service which is appropriate in some circumstances.

It is a good idea to have all applicants write a letter of application. This will reveal a lot about their language ability, personality, tidiness, accuracy and so forth. Then go through the letters and divide them into three piles: one for interviews, one for doubtful applications that you will hold, and one for those who are clearly unsuitable. The interviewing process is very difficult. If you are in the majority of small business operators who don't have the luxury of employing a specialised personnel manager, it is highly likely that you will have to do it yourself.

The selection process must measure three main things. Firstly, the person's ability to do the job and how much induction training and supervision they will need in order to achieve optimum performance. Secondly, given that duties and responsibilities do not remain constant, especially in the areas of technological and economic change, it must measure the applicant's experience and potential to learn new skills, to adapt to new methods and accept additional responsibilities, rather than relying solely on their training background. Thirdly, in order to permit detailed person-power planning and executive development, the selection process must measure a person's potential for advancement within the organisation and determine the special training he or she will need to be fully equipped for advancement.

Develop detailed questions to elicit this information and keep a check list to remind you of them. Allow enough time for the meeting and ensure that there is privacy. Determine what other techniques you are going to use. It may be an idea also to develop an application form which could encompass some of the questions just mentioned to be completed by the applicant.

It is important, then, to take time in the induction and training of new employees. Time spent with them when they first come to you, teaching them about the business and its goals and letting them read the relevant parts of the business plan, could be invaluable in the future. While they are fresh they may have better ideas on new perspectives, so you should give them enough confidence to talk freely to you and make constructive suggestions, even at this early stage.

Once you have recruited staff it is important to train them. Lack of training is the Achilles' heel of small business, despite the good intentions of the recently legislated Training Levy Scheme. There are many opportunities for training in Australia, including employer associations, TAFE colleges and the Small Business Development Corporation. Most of these courses are free or modestly priced. The real problem, then, is not the availability of training courses, but getting the small business community to recognise the benefits of such training. For attitudes to change, the importance of training must first be recognised in the schools. For example, all apprentices should be taught how their employers' businesses stay afloat. Training is a big investment, so make sure you gain an adequate return on it. Before you send any of your staff on a training course find out what the course is designed to teach them and accept that on their return they may suggest ideas for change. Employees should be encouraged to pass on what they have learned. It is good management practice to evaluate any completed training.

If your recruitment procedure fails in some way or an employee's circumstances change, and the employee decides to leave your company, you should have what is known as an 'exit interview'. The interview can be quite revealing about your own business. Ask why they are leaving, what could have been improved in the business to make their job more enjoyable or make them more efficient.

Of course you have the right to hire and fire, but it is wise not to fly off the handle and suddenly sack someone. It is much smarter to plan ahead. If you are contemplating dismissing an employee due to inefficiency or wrongdoing, such as suspected theft, then hold at least two meetings and document them. (Ideally you should both sign the document as a true record of the discussion.) In the first meeting tell the employee that they have one month to resolve the problem, otherwise they will have to go. Have the employee make certain undertakings which you will then review. If the undertakings haven't been met, the inefficiencies haven't been eliminated or the errors still occur then hold and document a second meeting (and a third, if it becomes necessary to dismiss the employee). Remember that the employee has every right to call on the Conciliation and Arbitration Commission to determine whether wrongful dismissal has occurred and perhaps whether they should be re-employed or compensation paid.

You must be mindful of the powers of the Industrial Relations Commission as well as the power of the unions in this regard. There are also wage guidelines for both the employer and the employee regarding payments to an employee on dismissal. These are prepared by a division of the Department of Labour which operates in every State. Should you, as an employer, have action brought against you then you can look to your various employer federations for guidance and help. These are member organisations, but they will also assist non-members.

If you have given adequate warning, preferably in writing, stating the problems and the action required by the employee, then you are on fairly safe ground. Be honest about it, document the process, give warnings, give the employee the chance to perform. If they don't perform after the chance is given, then dismiss them. There is no point in being a hero and trying to keep your people for humanity's sake or just because you are afraid of the possible complications of letting them go. It is better to be sharp and quick and to reduce overheads so that your business can survive and pay the remaining employees.

UNIONS

Like it or not, the union movement is entrenched in the Australian work-force. From the moment the first settlers' ships arrived here unions have increased in number and strength, encompassing all areas and industries and having varying degrees of power. A brief treatment of industrial relations in this country is therefore warranted here.

In business, particularly in the smaller businesses, the impact of unions may not always be directly felt because not all employees are members. Employees and employers who are not covered by the Federal Award are not, however, Award free. State Awards and Common Law Awards apply to all employees in the industries and occupations specified, which basically covers all employees. The Federal Conciliation and Arbitration Commission settles and deals with interstate disputes and often deals with intrastate matters, despite the lack of formal authority to do so. State and Federal tribunals operate concurrently, assisting the Government, the employees and the unions.

The Australian Conciliation and Arbitration Commission is charged with the responsibility of preventing and settling industrial disputes. The awards under which unions operate generally cover rates of pay; penalty rates; overtime; hours of work; special rates for special conditions: leave entitlements, sick, annual, long service leave; terms of employment, that is, termination of employment, payment and frequency of wages; rights of union officials; protective clothing and equipment; and allowances.

As a small business operator you must understand how the unions or the awards that cover your employees will affect you, not forgetting, of course, the impact the unions will have on the wider economy, particularly your suppliers and your customers. If your customers have union problems it will obviously affect their ability to order services or products from you. Similarly, your operations could be severely affected if your suppliers are unable to complete the manufacture of raw material for your business.

Like any institution the union movement has the potential for either advancing your business or disrupting its common ethics. How, then, do you develop a union management climate that directs this potential towards constructive ends? Unfortunately there is no simple or magic formula for achieving this overnight. Wisdom, sensitivity and hard work must be applied in showing that the union is accepted as a responsible part of the operation.

Owners will probably have most of their union contact with the shop steward. The shop steward or job delegate is an employee and an elected representative of the union. As such, he or she is recognised by fellow employees to be the official spokesperson for the union. This can be difficult because a shop steward must serve two bosses. As an employee the shop steward is expected to perform satisfactory work for you, the employer, by following orders and directions. As a union representative the shop steward has responsibilities to other employees and to the union. If the owner understands this dual role the shop steward can be allowed to create an effective link between the business and the employees.

A shop steward's role is generally spelt out in detail in the Awards that relate to each particular business or industry. But the part the shop steward plays depends largely on his or her personality. Some shop stewards are unassuming, others are overbearing. Some are helpful and courteous, others are militant and disruptive. Some will take advantage of their position and do as little work as possible, others will perform an excellent day's work in addition to their union duties.

Procedures should be adopted in the business to spell out in detail what is required of everybody and these should be passed around to all employees. Should a grievance or complaint occur the shop steward, accompanied by the affected employee, will usually present it. The owner should listen to both of them carefully. There is nothing to prohibit the owner from speaking directly with the employee in the presence of the shop steward. In other words, there should be free and open communication among the parties. It is in the owner's interest not to feel irritated or threatened by the employee's complaint. Obviously it is better to be close to the employee in the first place so that the complaint comes directly to you rather than going through the union.

When in doubt over union matters, don't panic. Consult with your employer associations; they have experts who deal with these matters. In the very early stages of a problem that you can't resolve amicably with the employee or shop steward, bring in your employer association. Get them to come out to your factory or business and see if they can render their help. They have the expertise — that is what you are paying your membership for — so make sure you utilise them in these important instances.

KEEPING THE BOOKS

We noted earlier that inexperience and incompetence go hand in hand to produce much small business failure, mainly through the management's inability to generate sales, limit expenses, collect debts and control investments in stock. And these problems are often compounded by a lack of administration skills or the straightforward ability to record and account for the daily, weekly and monthly transaction of the business.

Bookkeeping is often considered time consuming and tedious, but this is only true if a backlog is allowed to occur. When you decide to go into business open up a business bank account and keep it separate from your personal accounts. This will facilitate clear record keeping.

Good accounting habits do not protect a business against failure; however, they are an essential first step in helping to avoid some of the managerial problems which lead to collapse. Moreover, the information made available to small business proprietors by sound accounting records allows them to assess personal performance more competently, to apply for supplier credit and bank loans and to prepare taxation returns. It also serves as a basis for future planning and helps to protect business assets from carelessness, errors and fraud.

Some form of record keeping is essential for all business operations. The extent, nature and detail of records maintained will depend on the type of business information required, and should be subject to advice from your accountant (who might also be involved in setting up the records). Whatever records you keep, they must be meaningful and understandable. Unless you constantly refer to them, discuss what they show you and act on the conclusions you draw from them, they are useless.

Every system begins with two types of information: receipts (money received from business activities) and payments (money spent in running the business), which are recorded in the form of primary records. Deposit slips record money deposited in the bank, and cheque butts record most payments made. Where payments are made in cash, a cash sale docket or receipt should be provided by the entity making the sale and this becomes the primary record. It is from these records that entries are made to the receipts and payments journals, so it is essential that they are complete. Receipts should identify the:

- name of the customer,
- reason for receiving payment,
- amount received, and
- date of receipt.

Cheque butts should identify the:

- date payment is made,
- name of the entity to which payment is being made,
- reason for making the payment, and
- amount paid.

Additional records recommended for efficient bookkeeping include:

1 documents of various types
2 a cash journal
3 a bank reconciliation
4 a production record
5 a payroll record
6 a sales record
7 a petty cash record
8 a fixed asset record
9 accounting records,

as well as cashflow books, invoice books and wages books. We will treat some of them in detail.

1 Documents

The first accounting habit to develop is to support every transaction with a written record, however informal. These

127

might include sales dockets and receipts, cash register tapes, delivery notices and invoices, cheque stubs, payment advices and employee time sheets. These are the source documents which may be demanded by auditors, customers, suppliers and tax investigators as proof of transactions. With the recently introduced taxation substantiation requirements you must either keep a copy of the invoice/receipt supporting your income/payment or date and sign your cheque butt.

Procedures should be set up for storing and processing the documents that you will receive from other organisations, such as invoices from suppliers. These procedures need not be complicated. In fact, the simpler the procedure, the greater the chance that it will be used consistently. By establishing and adhering to a simple set of procedures for handling business documents the small business proprietor will find it easier to collect customer debts, pay suppliers and control levels of cash liquidity. The storage of source documents is also a matter which should be carefully considered and discussed with the accountant. Depending on your budget, the documents can be stored in anything from shoe boxes to elaborate commercial filing systems, on anything from loose sheets of paper to microfiche. Stationers supply box-and-ring files, specially designed card files and filing cabinets at reasonable prices, all of which are suitable for storing documents. Whatever means is selected, it should be logical, easy to operate, and protected from damage and misuse.

Some of the basic routines that should be considered when setting up the accounting framework for a small business are:

- a record and reconciliation of cash takings and sales for the day;
- a procedure to ensure that credit is extended only to authorised customers and within their agreed credit limit;
- a procedure to ensure customers are billed correctly and promptly for the goods they have received on credit;
- a procedure for receiving goods. Delivery notes or

packing slips should be checked against goods when delivered;

- a system of payment for goods and services. Do invoices agree with delivery notices? Are prices correct? Is the arithmetic correct? Even computer-generated accounts can be wrong, as can bank statements;
- a procedure for ensuring that staff are paid correctly. This will involve checking time sheets, pay rates, tax instalments and so on;
- a procedure to ensure that the inventory records relate to the physical stock on hand — that is, a stocktake.

The effectiveness of these procedures will be enhanced by segregating, wherever possible, the duties performed by employees of the business. For example, the employee who receives cash should not be responsible for reconciling it or banking it. The employee who receives incoming goods should not perform the stocktake alone or be responsible for payment of suppliers. In a small business it is not always possible to segregate all the duties, but you should seek to allocate tasks as sensibly as you can.

Many people are unfamiliar with the paperwork of business, are uncertain of the relationship between delivery notes, invoices and statements, and find it confusing to determine exactly how much they should pay for goods and services rendered. Generally, a delivery note is intended as a memorandum of goods received; an invoice is a detailed list of amounts charged for each item received and a record of accounts payable to the supplier; and the statement records the balance due, made up of the current invoices payable plus any balance payable from the previous months since the last statement was issued.

Learning how to match delivery notes with invoices and invoices with statements is not difficult. Advantages to be gained include: reducing the probability of under- or over-payment of accounts, allowing your business to gain valuable purchase discounts where available and protecting the business's credit reputation. Source documents such as these are evidence of transactions. Transactions must be recorded if they are to provide the information necessary for the purposes which are intended, such as measuring performance and adhering to the business plan.

2 Cash Journals

Well-kept cash records are essential for keeping track of the business cash resources. They also mean that your accountant can prepare reports and returns more quickly. Provided there is a concise record of all receipts and payments for any period, they eliminate the need for the accountant to analyse cheque stubs and receipt books — a time-consuming and error-prone task. They also provide a convenient breakdown of the various kinds of receipts and payments.

When you are starting off in business you should do your own manual cash journals and records. This is the only way you will know exactly how much money you are spending. It is one thing to write out cheques from time to time, but another to sit down and add them all up, reconcile them, cross-balance them to get the totals which show what is physically going out and what is physically coming in, and compare the two — money in versus money out.

Normally these cash records will have a date column; a column showing who the payment is to or from; a reference column which gives the source document — either a cheque stub or a receipt book number; the amount column, which should tally with the bank; and then various headings which make sense to the business. A good accounting habit is to record receipts and payments from their source documents into journals at regular intervals, say daily or weekly. If performed regularly the task is not onerous and allows a regular check to be made of the business's cash position.

The accuracy of the journals can be checked in two ways. Firstly, the total of all the breakdown columns should equal the total of the amount column. If there is any disagreement, check both to see that they have been completed properly. Secondly, a bank reconciliation should be completed each month on receipt of the bank statement, or more frequently if your cashflow requires, say daily or weekly. This provides a valuable check on the accuracy and completeness of the amounts shown in the journals as well as information on the state of the business's cash resources. It will also reveal any errors made by the bank.

There are various ways to record cash journals, computers being one way of hastening the process. But the owner/manager should really be involved personally. The design of the journals will be determined by the kind of transactions about which the business proprietor requires individual information. For instance, one proprietor may require to know the amount spent on petrol and oil as a separate amount from that which is spent on motor vehicle repairs. Hence, his or her financial report should show two separate amounts relating to motor vehicles. If these are regular kinds of expenses then it makes sense to design a cash journal whose dissection column includes a column for petrol and oil and a column for vehicle repairs. The business proprietor should discuss in detail with his or her accountant those transactions which are to be collected as individual data and those which are to be reported as individual amounts. From these discussions the accountant will probably draw up a chart of recommended headings for the different dissections.

3 Bank Reconciliation

Many small businesses leave this in the hands of their accountant but there are real advantages in the proprietor doing it her/himself at least monthly or more often. By maintaining cash journals like those discussed it is very easy for the small business proprietor to form his or her own bank reconciliations.

The business's cash balance in its own records is the difference between the total of its cash receipts and the total of its cash payments. If cash receipts are greater than cash payments the cash balance is favourable. If payments exceed receipts your business is in trouble, unless there is an overdraft arrangement with the bank. The balance of the cash account is determined by taking the previous balance and adding to it the total receipts for the period as per the cash receipt journal, then subtracting the total cash payments for the period as per the cash payment journal. Sometimes this will vary because there will be a time lag between cheques being sent out and being presented at the bank. Therefore, adjustments have to be made for this. Also, deposits that have gone through the cash book may not necessarily appear on the bank statements yet. Again adjustments have to be made. Thirdly, charges levied by the bank and sometimes periodical payments that you have authorised for, say, leasing must also be noted in the cash journals. A reconciliation is thus achieved between what is shown in your cash books and what is shown in the bank statements.

It is also important to check your figures in your cash book against the bank statement figures to ensure that the amounts have been recorded accurately in the cash book, or, indeed, that a cheque has been written out accurately. Similarly, on the cash receipts, you have to make sure the bank pay-in slip is accurately recorded in the cash receipts journal. Checking off each receipt or payment in the cash book as they are discovered on the bank statement is a simple matter to determine outstanding deposits and cheques and to check that the bank has not made any mistakes. (Banks are certainly not infallible. In my early accounting days in the country, we discovered, in the course of doing a client's taxation return six months after the event, that more than $100,000 worth of wheat cheques had gone into the account of someone else with the same surname and first initial!)

In summary, the steps for recording a bank reconciliation are as follows:

- Review the bank statements for fees, charges and periodical payments and adjust the cash books as necessary.
- Compare the bank deposits with the receipts in the cash receipt book and increase the bank statement balance by the total of the outstanding deposits.
- Compare the cheques paid by the bank with those listed in the cash payments book and decrease the

adjusted bank statement balance by the total of the outstanding cheques.

- Determine the balance of the cash account according to the cash books and make amendments if necessary.

4 Production Records

For manufacturing businesses, production records aid in job costing. They allow the business proprietor to determine the labour and material costs of products and to compare them with expectations. When adequately designed and well kept these records are an important source of information for the business.

5 Payroll records

The sole business proprietor has a legal obligation to the taxation authorities to maintain adequate payroll records. If registered as a group employer, the small business proprietor is obliged to deduct tax instalments from employees' wages and to pay group tax on a monthly or regular basis to the Australian Taxation Office. Payroll records provide a basis for meeting these obligations. Furthermore, the employer is required to issue group certificates to employees each year showing the amount of tax that has been deducted from their salaries. Payroll records allow this to be performed accurately and promptly.

6 Sales Records

Some businesses may find it impossible to assess performance and plan future operations without keeping a record of sales figures for different areas.

7 Petty Cash Records

It is usual to keep a small amount of cash on hand for the payment of petty or minor expenses, such as stamps, newspapers, coffee, tea and so on. Such money should not be taken from the cash register. It should be kept separately and recorded and balanced daily or weekly. The use of 'IOU' vouchers should be discouraged.

8 Fixed Asset Record

A fixed asset record is often required by the accountant for vehicles and other office equipment and plant. Usually he or she will require from the client the cost of any fixed assets purchased during the period, the amounts received for any assets sold during the period, as well as the date when such purchases or sales occurred. This also applies to other asset records, such as shares and investments which may be held in the business name.

9 Accounting Records

From the accounting records of the business the accountant will produce financial reports (see pages 153–6). Sadly, the only use made of these reports by many business owners is for the preparation of tax and company returns. Yet, as stated earlier, they provide important data for assessing the performance of the business in order to plan future operations and, as will be seen, to identify any problems, especially when generated more than once a year.

Other important records include:

- accounts receivable (debtors), which records who owes you money, how old the debt is and how much (a simple card system will do, summarised on a page with lists of customers who owe you money and amounts dissected into days or months outstanding);
- an inventory or stock record (again a card system will suffice if computers are not cost effective);
- accounts payable — that is, creditors (a well-organised set of paid and unpaid accounts from creditors is often sufficient for business to control payment of their accounts; however, a card or equivalent system may also be used and summarised on one piece of paper, showing all the creditors listed and the age of the outstanding amounts added up).

COSTING AND PRICING

Remember the ingredients for success: there's no point in making a sale unless you profit and collect. Costing and pricing are very important in this equation.

Too many people in business don't know what their activities are costing them. They manufacture something, they sell it and they don't even add up the costs of the materials they used to make it. Even if they do include materials, they forget their own labour. Or, if they remember both of these, they undervalue them. They also forget about rent, overheads, wages, government charges and levies. They forget to include the interest on borrowed money. When it comes to calculating their selling price they are motivated only by making a sale.

Costing, more than anything else, seems to frighten off people in small business. Most are more interested in the production of their article than the correct costing of it. Whilst many successful enterprisers rely on their noses to arrive at a selling price, today's fierce competition and high costs underline the necessity of ensuring that each item is properly costed. Inflation also plays a role here. Today's products must be costed to allow for today's expenses. Some basic knowledge of costing is therefore essential. To maximise profit the owner must understand the different types of costs and how they behave.

So, what does my product/service cost me? There are three aspects to this. The real costs to any business are firstly its labour cost, particularly your own, secondly the cost of external borrowings, and finally other fixed and variable costs.

The Small Business Development Corporation outlines the following steps towards calculating an hourly labour rate:

STEP 1 Calculate the **total actual cost of labour**:

Gross wage of employee @ $320 per week	$16,640 p.a.
ADD payroll tax (if applicable) @ 5%	$ 832
ADD holiday pay loading @ 17.5% of holiday pay	$ 224
ADD workers' compensation premium	$ 800
Total actual labour cost	$18,496

135

STEP 2 Calculate the **total hours available**:

Available time = 5 days per week × 52 weeks	260 days

LESS holiday @ 4 weeks per annum	20 days
LESS sick days @ 5 days per annum	5 days
LESS public holidays @ 10 days per annum	10 days
LESS long service leave @ approx. 5 days per annum	5 days

Total days available	220 days

STEP 3 Calculate **total productive hours per annum** by multiplying daily productive hours (assuming an eight-hour day with one unproductive hour) by total days available:

7 hours × 220 days = 1540 hours per annum

STEP 4 Calculate **cost of labour** by dividing total actual cost by total productive hours per annum:

$$\frac{\$18,496}{1540} = \$12$$

STEP 5 Calculate the **overhead rate per direct labour hour** by dividing estimated manufacturing overheads by estimated direct labour hours:

For the purposes of this illustration assume $6 per hour.

STEP 6 Calculate the **labour rate** by adding the result of Step 4 to the result of Step 5:

$12 + $6 = $18

STEP 7 Calculate the **mark-up on the labour rate** as shown in Step 6 (Assume 25% mark-up):

25% of $18 = $4.50

STEP 8 Calculate the **charge-out rate** by adding mark-up to labour rate:

$4.50 + $18 = $22.50

Even if you do not have staff, you still have labour costs — your own. In calculating what you are worth to your business, consider what you would be paid for doing this sort of work elsewhere. Don't forget to allow for annual leave, that is, four weeks' wages plus 17.5% loading, or the equivalent in overtime.

The second aspect of costing is the cost of external borrowings (that is, interest and fees) and any dividends to be paid to external investors. The most common form of external borrowing for businesses is bank overdraft and the cost can fairly readily be determined by looking at the charges that come through on a monthly or quarterly basis on your bank statements. Also in this category are the interest costs on personal loans, fully drawn advances, mortgages, and so on. Perhaps with the help of your accountant, you should be able to calculate the cost of these loans, as well as any other costs and interest charges in hire purchase and leasing arrangements.

Finally, assess your fixed costs and variable costs and how they affect your profit margin. Fixed costs are the cost of staying in business and do not vary with sales levels. They include: rent, insurance, telephone, possibly other expenses and also interest charged on hire purchase agreements or leasing charges for all capital equipment used in the business. Variable costs are the costs that vary with turnover or production. The most important of these is the cost of raw materials (or of goods sold, in retailing) and the labour content of the business where it is directly related to production or sales. The less important variable costs may be car-running expenses, power, and so on.

It is the balance between fixed and variable costs that makes for the profitability of the business and these factors are used to calculate the break-even point, or the level of output at which total sales equals total costs of the business. The break-even point can readily be calculated by dividing fixed costs by the so-called 'contribution' (sales revenue minus variable costs) per unit. The result indicates how many items must be sold to make neither a profit nor a loss for a particular year. The break-even point can be lowered by decreasing fixed costs, decreasing variable costs, increasing selling price or a combination of all three. It is very useful for planning purposes.

Break-even is absolutely critical, no matter how small or

large your business is. Obviously the bigger the business, the more sophisticated the system needed to calculate it. In a small business you should know, on a day-by-day basis, exactly how many sales are required to make a profit. You should know what your overheads and fixed costs are, on which day of the week you have made a profit or a loss, on which day you have broken even and when you will start to make a profit. Do you have sufficient sales by the Thursday, so that Friday and Saturday morning, if you are in a retail business, are profitable? There is no business that cannot be broken down on a weekly or daily basis. If you cannot do this then you haven't done your costing properly and you haven't calculated your break-even properly. And if you don't make the profits you should make then you are probably going to go broke.

A number of factors govern the appropriate pricing of goods or services, but basically prices must cover all costs, both variable (those that change with numbers sold) and fixed (those that don't change, regardless of turnover). There must be a return to the owner which reflects the risk, effort and money invested. Other factors to be considered are:

- pricing policies of competitors;
- price sensitivity of the product or service (will higher prices result in customers switching to other suppliers?);
- price consciousness of customers (is the target market more interested in price, or quality?);
- the level of overhead costs to be covered.

Specials — offering certain products or services at low prices — can be used to induce customers to visit the business. Cutting prices is often advisable for slow-moving or redundant stock/services.

Selling on credit can often increase sales and might be necessary for big-ticket items, for businesses dependent upon cyclical income received by their customers (for example, country stores dependent on the custom of farmers) or for businesses whose customers need to make regular (say, monthly) purchases (for example, pharmacists).

So, what is the best selling price? In setting prices the goal must simply be to maximise profit, not to maximise sales. Although some operators feel that increased sales volume is needed for increased profit, volume alone does not mean more profit. Profit is made up of three ingredients: cost, selling price and the unit sales volume. The desired profit is achieved by adjusting the respective proportions of these. No one pricing formula will produce a greater profit under all conditions. Up-to-date knowledge of market conditions is also necessary because the 'right' selling price for a product under one set of market conditions may be the wrong price at other times. The best selling price for a product is not necessarily the price that will sell the most units, nor is it always the price that will bring in the greatest number of sale dollars. Rather, the best price is the one that will maximise the profit of the company. The best selling price should be cost-orientated and market-orientated. It should be high enough to cover your costs and make a profit for you. It should be low enough to attract customers and build sales volume.

The most common form of pricing by small business owners is mark-up pricing, as distinct from demand. This system uses the cost of the product or service as a base and then adds a mark-up, usually a percentage, to this base. Mark-up is not the same as gross profit margin. Gross profit margin is always less than the mark-up. However, it is extremely important for small business to know and understand the concept of gross profit margin (and how it differs from mark-up) because it is this proportional percentage of each dollar from sales which is used to pay overheads, wages and taxes, establish reserves and provide a return to the owner. To calculate the gross profit margin all you need to know is the percentage mark-up.

Pricing really comes back to what the market will wear. Often you are better off to charge a higher price. For example, if you quote $1200 instead of $1000, and if your customers feel they are getting good value, then you would have been foolish to quote the lower price, even though the item only cost you half of that. If competition occurs or other factors come into it you can always bring the price down. I know this notion is hard to come to grips with, but I really do think you should never undercharge. You should, if anything, overcharge.

CASE STUDY:

I know a solicitor who studied accounting with me before doing Law at Melbourne University. He started as a small practitioner in a smart office in the city with one staff member and a huge library. I wanted to set up my own company trust but, in those early days, didn't know much about how it was done, so I went to him out of loyalty. He charged me twice as much as anyone else would have, and it was only his first year out. What is more, before I even had a chance to complain he was taking steps to collect his money and threatening to sue.

Today that bloke is a lecturer in Law, has properties in London and Australia, has successfully floated two public companies, is an expert adviser on the board of several major legal firms and works about a quarter of the hours I do. I guess he had it right from day one. He believes in his product, he believes in himself, he's charged the maximum and he's collected his money.

It is worth reiterating here the importance of the opportunity cost, or the value of your own money. If that money were not tied up in the business you could be investing it and earning 10, 12 or 15 per cent (the going market rate) or you could be putting it into property and earning something that way. Consider what effect it would have on the net profit of the business if you charged, say, 12.5 per cent for the use of money you have invested in the business. Is there any compensating growth in the goodwill of the business so that if you sold out you would make a capital gain? Look at the net profit of the business before taking account of your own labour and the effect of charging interest on your own money invested. Then deduct these expenses to arrive at an adjusted net profit figure. Are you left with any profit? If you are left with the figure you expected, you must weigh up the non-financial advantage of continuing and then decide whether your business makes adequate use of your labour and the money you have invested.

CASE STUDY:

Stuart had a small automotive workshop with lots of sophisticated equipment. He had an established client base, but he never made any money. He was working formidable hours, usually starting at 6.00 a.m. and not finishing until 10.00 p.m. He worked six and a half days a week. The rest of the time he worried about the business and wondered why he wasn't making any money.

We went and did a small analysis of his business and witnessed some major strengths — established client base, good location, good equipment (if anything too much) — and only one weakness: too much stock tying up his cashflow. Then we found out that he was barely charging out his own labour and he was just covering the cost of his materials. He wasn't keeping accurate wage records and had no labour time records at all.

We advised him to increase his prices. The thought was inconceivable to him because the business had been his father's for many years and he didn't want to upset anybody. Eventually, after many discussions and the re-calculation of his costs, we talked him into increasing his prices — by two hundred per cent!

He kept his materials at cost, with a small mark-up for packaging and travel, and charged correctly for labour. To his amazement, the only customers he lost were bad payers anyway, so he was better off without them. His profits dramatically increased, he had more time to spend at home with his six kids, he could have the holiday he had always looked forward to, and he could assist his parents, who weren't very well off. He was a new person.

Often in hard times small businesses see a reduction in sales without a change in margins. How do you cope with this? Well, you have got to try to reduce your fixed costs by re-evaluating your product and services and perhaps discarding unprofitable lines. Guard against an in-built view that a particular line cannot be cut out. Call in somebody else (your mentor or an accountant) to analyse the situation objectively; you might be surprised to see that the bottom line return comes from another line altogether.

Increase your margin if products or services are not price sensitive. Consider decreasing your direct cost by obtaining greater discounts or substituting cheaper material stocks. You should also reduce your stock levels to cope with the cost pressures and reduction in sales.

Any decrease in sales will cause a loss in revenue which will also decrease your working capital. One way to cope with decreasing sales is to in fact decrease your prices and run sales on slow-moving stock. Reassess and reduce your borrowings to reduce interest paid on borrowed funds. Check cost efficiencies, especially fixed costs, to offset squeezed profit margins. Reassess capacity needs and if necessary dispose of surplus assets, equipment, staff and stock. The best strategy for increasing profits is to increase volume, to improve profitability and to reduce expenses.

BUDGETING

It is very important in business to know where you are going and how to get there, in other words to make a forecast in the form of a budget.

Budgets have many uses. They assist in communicating to you, your bank manager and key personnel the cost and overall charges involved in your planned operation. The budgeting process provides a benchmark against which actual performance can be measured, thus serving to motivate, to set targets, and to encourage the delegation of responsibility. Budgeting can be used for forecasting, for planning, and for controlling. Depending on the type and size of the operation, some or all of the following may be necessary: a sales budget; a production budget; a profit and loss statement; and, of course, as we have seen, the all-important cash budget.

Budgets, however, must not be rigid; they must be flexible enough to cater not only for controllable costs but also for those beyond control. They must also allow for sales or production fluctuations.

Part of the budgeting process is to determine the break-even point. As we have seen, break-even is the point at which sales volume, in numbers and dollars, covers the fixed expenses of the business and you start to make a profit. Profits result from selling goods and services at a price high enough to enable the business to pay all expenses, including the cost of goods sold, and to have a surplus remaining. The break-even chart is often a useful tool to combine with your budget, as it reveals useful ratios.

It is important to complete the budget before the financial year begins, even though the actual results of the previous year will not be known in precise detail. If this is not done the discipline of performance measurement will lapse in the first month of the year. If the monthly reporting procedure described on pages 153–9 is in operation then the production of annual accounts should not give rise to any surprises.

The budget should be prepared and constantly reviewed by those responsible for achieving it, using the past as the best guide to the future. In practice, the budgeting process will normally start with last year's achievement. The figures will then be adjusted to reflect planned changes. Even in a stable business, adjustments will have to be made for inflation, expected wage settlements and changing interest rates. The main weakness of this approach is perpetuating the mistakes of the past. For an expanding business these mistakes can be multiplied. It is a good idea to attempt to prepare budgets from square one. This technique is known as zero-based budgeting. It is a useful device for examining the business objectively and questioning established procedures. If you have ambitious expansion plans, then zero-based budgets may be the best alternative.

Despite the critical importance of turnover, ('bums on seats', in the case of restaurants), many small businesses find it

Cashflow Budget — International Products Inc.

	JULY	AUG.	SEPT.	OCT.	NOV.	DEC.	JAN.
SALES - PROCESSING	3500	3800	4000	4000	3900	3400	3500
- PHOTOGRAPHY	2000	2800	3000	3000	2200	1000	1500
- PRINTER	8000	10000	15000	15000	12000	6000	7000
- GRAPHICS	64500	89900	129000	126000	103400	53600	59500
- FILM	2000	3500	4000	5000	4500	1000	1500
- OTHER	10000	20000	25000	27000	24000	5000	7000
TOTAL SALES	90000	130000	180000	180000	150000	70000	80000
LESS COST OF GOODS SOLD							
OPENING STOCK							
SUB-CONTRACTORS							
PURCHASES	22500	32500	45000	45000	37500	17500	20000
PHOTOGRAPHY							
PROCESSING							
OTHER							
WORK IN PROGRESS MOVEMENT							
COST OF GOODS SOLD (25%)	22500	32500	45000	45000	37500	17500	20000
GROSS PROFIT	67500	97500	135000	135000	112500	52500	60000
SELLING EXPENSES							
ADVERTISING & PROMOTION	1000	4000	4000	2000	1000	500	500
ENTERTAINMENT	40	40	40	40	40	40	40
EXHIBITIONS/TRADE FAIRS				6000			
TRAVEL/ACC./O'SEAS	310	310	310	310	310	310	310
BROCHURSE/PRINTING	3000			2000			
ADMINISTRATION & GENERAL							
AUDIT & ACCOUNTING				1259			
LEGAL EXPENSES							500
POWER - LIGHT				1000			
CLEANING	20	20	20	20	20	20	20
INSURANCE			2700			1500	
MOTOR VEHICLE EXPS.	1800	1800	1800	2000	1800	1800	1800
INSURANCE - WORKCARE	1301.4	1440	1440	1440	1440	1440	1476
LONG SERVICE LEAVE	143	143	143	143	143	143	150
SERVICE CONTRACTS	3000	3000	3000	3000	3000	3000	3000
RATES							
REPAIRS & MAINTENANCE				1000		1000	2000
SALARIES & WAGES	14460	16000	16000	16000	16000	16000	16400
STAFF AMENITIES	50	50	50	50	50	50	50
TELEPHONE	1000	850	2000	1000	1200	500	2000
RENT PAID	1921	1921	1921	1921	1921	1921	1921
SUPERANNUATION	500	500	500	500	500	500	500
FINANCIAL EXPENSES							
BAD & DOUBTFUL DEBTS							
BANK CHARGES & INTEREST	300	300	300	300	300	300	300
DEBT COLLECTION EXP.							
INTEREST - OTHER &							
LEASE PAYMENTS	12176	12176	12176	12176	12176	12176	12176
LOAN REPAYMENT					20000	20000	20000
TOTAL EXPENSES	41021.4	42550	46400	52159	59900	61200	63143
NET CASH POSITION	26478.6	54950	88600	82841	52600	-8700	-3143
CUMULATIVE	26478.6	81428.6	170028.6	252869.6	305469.6	296769.6	293626.6

144

FEB.	MARCH	APRIL	MAY	JUNE	TOTAL	YEAR TWO	YEAR THREE
3700	4000	4000	3900	3700	45400	68033	88443
2000	3000	2500	2450	2000	27450	41000	53320
9000	15000	13000	13000	11000	134000	200843	261100
87300	129000	112750	115150	99800	1169900	1754850	2281300
3000	4000	3750	3500	3500	39250	58900	76600
15000	25000	24000	22000	20000	224000	336374	437237
120000	180000	160000	160000	140000	1640000	2460000	31980000
					0		
30000	45000	40000	40000	35000	410000	615000	799500
					0		
30000	45000	40000	40000	35000	410000	615000	799500
90000	135000	120000	120000	105000	1230000	1845000	2398500
					0		
1000	4000	3000	2000	500	23500	7000	8000
40	40	40	40	40	480	550	640
		7000			13000	18000	24000
			18000		18000	22000	26000
310	310	310	310	310	3720	4600	4800
	2000				7000	10000	12000
					0		
					0		
1250					2509	2759.9	3035.89
					500	550	605
		1000			2000	2200	2420
20	20	20	20	20	240	360	400
		1000			5200	5720	6292
1800	1800	1800	2000	1800	22000	26000	35000
1476	1674	1674	1674	1674	18149.4	19964.34	21960.77
150	150	150	150	150	1758	1933.8	2127.18
3000	3000	3000	3000	3000	36000	39600	43560
		1375			1375	1512.5	1663.75
	500			1000	5500	6050	6655
16400	18600	18600	18600	18600	201660	221826	244008.6
					0		
50	50	50	50	50	600	660	726
10000	1500	2000	1000	15000	38050	41855	46040.5
1921	1921	1921	1921	1921	23052	25357.2	27892.92
500	500	500	500	500	6000	6600	7260
					0		
					0		
					0		
300	300	300	300	300	3600	4400	4600
					0		
					0		
12176	12176	12176	12176	12176	146112	75000	15000
50000	40000	50000	50000	50000	300000	364200	
100393	88541	105916	111741	107041	880005.4	908698.7	544687.6
-10393	46459	14084	8259	-2041	349994.6	936301.2	1853812
283233.6	329692.6	343776.6	352035.6	349994.6			

impossible to estimate and therefore have trouble preparing budgets. This difficulty can be overcome with flexible budgeting, or the process of estimating sales turnover at various levels and preparing for it.

It is important that estimates be verified from time to time and certainly more regularly than annually. Many poor estimates will become apparent from reviewing the management reports themselves, whilst others will be corrected the following month when facts are known.

By comparing the monthly results with the budget you are appraising your performance in implementing the plans. Do not, however, waste time explaining any small difference that arises each month. Trends must be observed and explanations obtained for continuing variations. Remember, the purpose of comparison is not to amuse your accountant, but to enable management to identify action required to maintain or improve business performance. This is why you need management reporting systems. If they do not assist the decision-making process then the system or the management must be changed.

Obviously, if variations occur, such as a blow-out in an expense item, then greater control and pruning are required. But even an increase in sales over budget may not be in the best interests of the business if it is due to a windfall which will not be repeated, while in fact traditional sales have severely declined. Therefore your budgets (and financial reports) need to be detailed enough to detect any unusual occurrences so that immediate corrective action can be taken.

To summarise: budgeting provides a realistic estimate of income and costs for a given period and the financial situation at the end of that period. The budget should be designed to:

- enable the result of your business operations to be measured (separate budgets will probably be needed for sales, production costs and overheads);
- show sufficient details to allow significant variation from budget to be identified;
- avoid any confusion regarding responsibility for each section of the budget;

- meet the profit targets determined;
- be compatible with your reporting systems, so that you understand it sufficiently to act in a timely fashion.

Budgets are the basis on which to make sound business decisions as changes occur and on which to make comparisons between budget and actual results. By analysis of the result you can pinpoint where the estimates went wrong and can make decisions and enact strategies to correct the problems and/or capitalise on opportunities. Budgets provide a basis on which to make day-to-day decisions during the set period, and a guide to management for setting reasonable targets and objectives.

CASHFLOW — THE LIFEBLOOD

Cashflow is the lifeblood of any business, and like the blood in your veins it must be kept in circulation. If you are cut, and blood flows out and cannot be stemmed, you will eventually die. It is the same in a business. If costs go uncontrolled, if you don't move the cash around, the business dies — it is as simple as that. Cash is the main element of working capital and it behoves management to ensure that the business trades within its cash cycle. The cause of many insolvencies can be traced to poor understanding of the need for adequate cash to pay the bills.

Today most lenders realise that the key to successful financing and lending is accurate and tight cashflow. They usually look for evidence of this in realistic forecasts prepared by prudent and careful business owners showing precise management of stock, debtors and creditors.

In times of inflation, availability of finance is restricted by the overall increased demand and restrictions on credit. At the same time, interest rates are higher and this further compounds the problem. Inflation boosts the extra cash required by businesses due to the need to replace stock which costs more than the original stock. Many expenses run at high levels and there is a push-pull effect of creditors seeking earlier settlement in contrast to debtors wishing to settle much later. The result, of course, is a reduction in cash in hand. This forces up borrowing and further rations the capital required for expansion. If this is not available from external sources the company reserves are diminished.

A common failing amongst small business people, particularly in contracting or in businesses where payment is received up front, is the belief that cash in hand equates to profit. When cash is freely available they go out and spend it on peripheral items, non-essentials. On the day of reckoning they are in all sorts of trouble. You must manage cash prudently and estimate in advance how much cash is required. This can be achieved through the cashflow budget forecast. Where a surplus occurs, it can be invested to earn interest for future needs. Where shortages are anticipated you have sufficient advance notice to plan and investigate borrowing and its alternatives. Hard-core expenses can be planned, particularly those of a capital nature or involving an increase in stock. Rapidly rising cost trends can be observed and spending planned accordingly. Policy related to extent and timing of purchases and terms related to credit given and credit anticipated can also be carefully considered.

For small businesses, cars, plant and equipment are among the major capital expenditure items. Typical mistakes in this area are the purchasing of plant with excessive capacity, purchasing too many assets, premature acquisition of land and buildings, purchasing equipment which commits the business to out-of-date, unsuitable or uneconomical methods of production, or purchasing equipment (for example, motor vehicles) because they are tax deductible. Will the machine itself or the articles it produces become obsolete in the short term? What finance is required to purchase the asset? The decision on capital expenditure must be very carefully considered in the business plan.

Another potential drain on cashflow is the holding of too much stock. Many people starting out in business are seduced by the persuasive powers of sales people offering discounts and bulk purchase deals. But remember, stock is unrealised sales, it is cash sitting on the shelves or in the warehouse. I always say, if it doesn't sell it is very expensive. That is the reason why people go broke — they have too much stock or the wrong sort of stock.

Imagine your stock to be twenty-dollar notes. How carefully would you look at it then? If you fail to control your stock in the long run it will be dollars that you will be losing. Stock control simply involves being aware, by whatever method you find most convenient, of the level and condition at any time of anything purchased or manufactured by your business. This control should start much earlier than most businesses realise and should not finish until the goods have finally been converted into hard cash. Simple forms of control can be devised according to the needs of the business. Stock cards will normally suffice. Minimum and maximum levels should be set, as well as quantity to be reordered when the lower level is reached. These figures will naturally depend on usage, as well as the time it takes to obtain new supplies. A careful balance is needed between the danger of running short and the expense of overstocking.

Money tied up in stock is not working to the benefit of the business. Apart from the actual cost of buying required stock (whether raw materials or part-finished or completed goods), other expenses are involved. It is estimated that merely holding stock can cost up to twenty per cent of its basic value. Other costs can include holding charges, interest costs, losses or damage, obsolescence, handling, paperwork and so on. Nowadays, most multinational companies do not carry stock at all. They work on an automatic computer buying system to bring in their raw material stock from outside parties once an order has been received.

Stock turnover has a considerable effect on profitability, particularly in retailing, where a high proportion of funds are employed in financing stock. Stock turnover in these types of businesses is the hard core that truly spins the cash cycle. Gross profit margin dollars accumulate in direct proportion to how frequently the stock is being turned over or how hard this part of the working capital area is working.

Such is the critical importance of cashflow that many a small business operator spends more time fighting a rear-guard action with creditors than he or she does managing the business. This form of preoccupation is like a disease, but it need not be terminal.

As we have already noted, creditors are often one of the major sources of short-term funds for the smaller company. Although they appear as a liability in the financial statements, in fact, friendly creditors are a valuable asset even when trading is normal. When times get tough and you need the additional finance or cashflow, a friendly creditor can allow you to extend your terms for payment, and to survive.

We also saw earlier in this book what an important role the collection of debts plays in maintaining the cashflow of a business. Debt collection has a stronger-than-usual tendency to fail in hard times, with former 30-day payers taking 60, 90 or even 120 days because of their own cashflow problems.

Another potential drain on cashflow is the proprietor who takes too much out for personal use. You may be tempted to reward yourself for all your hard work by taking an overseas trip or buying an expensive car. But a substantial proportion of the business's profits should be retained in the business for increased working capital needs — to finance equipment and the inevitable growth of stock and debtors as your business expands — and, particularly in difficult times, to put away funds as a buffer. Remember, if the business is your main source of income then you and your income are interdependent. You need to ensure the security and future of both.

When a business is short of cash it is *undercapitalised*. This means that the total funds available to run the business are inadequate for the efficient conduct of the business. If that is the case the business becomes too dependent on its creditors. Undercapitalisation or insufficient working capital leads to the following losses and inefficiencies:

- a missed opportunity to purchase materials offered at a favourable price;
- the need to get rid of stock at an unprofitable price simply to obtain badly needed cash;
- the inability to afford sufficient materials to keep the production line running or to replace plant and equipment;

- constant distraction by day-to-day money problems, instead of concentrating on the business operations (management by crisis, not management by objectives).

Businesses that are undercapitalised can run into difficulties from circumstances entirely out of the manager's control, let alone the problem of actually going broke due to an inability to pay current liabilities. The main thing is to keep your financiers satisfied.

If, on the other hand, the business is overcapitalised, with more than sufficient funds to finance both its fixed and working capital, the issue will arise as to what to do with the excess. Surplus cash should be put to work immediately in order to generate additional funds. Before making investments that can tie up surplus cash for long periods it is advisable for small business owners to set aside a cash reserve that can be withdrawn quickly to meet any unforeseen contingency. Interest-bearing deposits with banks and building societies are a popular parking spot for such reserves.

Control of payments is also of prime importance. They should be made on the due dates, not before and certainly not after. If cash discounts are taken on accounts payable the procedure should be aimed towards eliminating the life of discounts due to clerical inefficiencies.

In summary, the small business person can optimise cash availability by accelerating collections, effecting payments on due dates, having few bank accounts and studying cashflows, including the relationship between cashflow and bank balances. In hard economic times, when one needs to live with borrowings, the manager of any highly geared company must ensure that the cashflow provides for all maturing liabilities and the interest on borrowed funds. Above all you must know your exact cash position (i.e. liquidity) at every moment of every day, particularly in hard times. You must know where your cash is and how much is available. You must know exactly what your bank balance is — overdraft or credit — based on the assumption that all dispatched cheques have been banked. A simple exercise book will serve to document this.

Some additional ways to improve your cashflow are:

1 Utilise a credit card system for customer payments. It is better than the company carrying its own accounts receivable.

2 Send out invoices as soon as the goods or services have been supplied. Set priorities for preparing invoices. If all invoices cannot be promptly mailed try to process the biggest amounts first.

3 Ask for up-front payment of part of the bill — in other words, a retainer. Some businesses are also in the position to bill on an interim basis.

4 Charge interest on delinquent accounts. (Note that in some States the customer may be required to sign an agreement to this effect before any demand for interest becomes binding.)

5 Convert to a 'pay on invoice only' system; in other words, drop the habit of sending out monthly statements. It only costs money and allows the customer extra time to pay the debt.

6 Arrange to send orders and invoices before the end of the month. An invoice dated 30 June will be paid earlier than one dated 1 July.

7 Sell on shorter terms (for example, payment required in 14 days rather than 30) and follow up earlier.

8 Drop small customers who don't pay promptly. Focus on large customers who pay on time.

9 Guard against selling to customers who are in financial difficulties. Be alert to any radical changes in buying or repayment behaviour.

Finally, when managing your cashflow, you should constantly be looking for better ways to borrow money or finance any current debt. Be ever vigilant. Superior cashflow management is clearly an essential art, for cashflow is a vital component of both corporate performance and its measurement — profit. For many it is the critical factor.

PUTTING IT ALL ON PAPER

Closely connected to the importance of budgeting and cashflow forecasting is the need to 'report' the business — in other words, to record its day-to-day activities. Recording takes the stress and the chance out of running a business and replaces these with control. Your records should always be kept current, as they can be rather tedious to update retrospectively.

Your accountant will advise you on the specific types of records you should keep, depending on the needs of your business. As we have seen, the main ones are the cash book, which records all cash entries, including cheques and payments; the sales and purchases record, which records payment to creditors and sales to customers; a record of your assets; and other sundry records. All these records are then used to prepare financial statements, or numerical representations of your efforts, your mistakes, your achievements — your blood, sweat and tears.

As I have said, no matter what financial statements a small business uses, the important thing is to actually understand them. We have already covered basic bookkeeping methods, but it is one thing to have the information at hand and another to be able to read it. It is no good having your accountant or bookkeeper prepare sophisticated profit and loss statements and balance sheets if you don't look at them or if you do look at them but don't understand them.

Apart from the cashflow statement, which we have already mentioned, the two most common types of financial statement are:
1 the profit and loss statement;
2 the balance sheet.

The profit and loss statement for a business is the measure of its profitability. The income, or sales revenue, represents your market — what you have sold, how much you have sold, at what price. Expenses, which come next after sales, represent what you spent to earn those sales — that is, what money has

(*Dollar amounts in thousands)

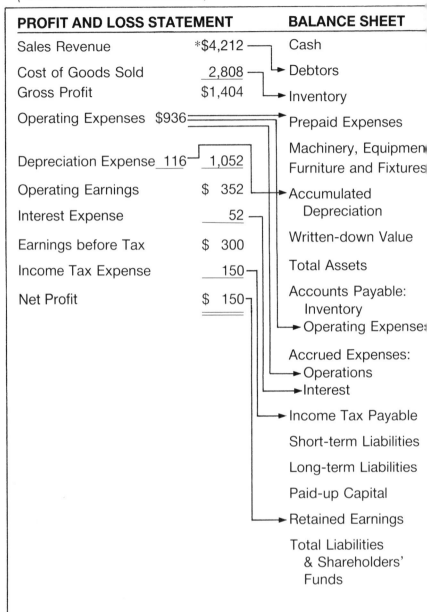

PROFIT AND LOSS STATEMENT		BALANCE SHEET
Sales Revenue	*$4,212	Cash
Cost of Goods Sold	2,808	Debtors
Gross Profit	$1,404	Inventory
Operating Expenses $936		Prepaid Expenses
		Machinery, Equipment Furniture and Fixtures
Depreciation Expense 116	1,052	
Operating Earnings	$ 352	Accumulated Depreciation
Interest Expense	52	Written-down Value
Earnings before Tax	$ 300	Total Assets
Income Tax Expense	150	Accounts Payable: Inventory Operating Expenses
Net Profit	$ 150	Accrued Expenses: Operations Interest
		Income Tax Payable
		Short-term Liabilities
		Long-term Liabilities
		Paid-up Capital
		Retained Earnings
		Total Liabilities & Shareholders' Funds

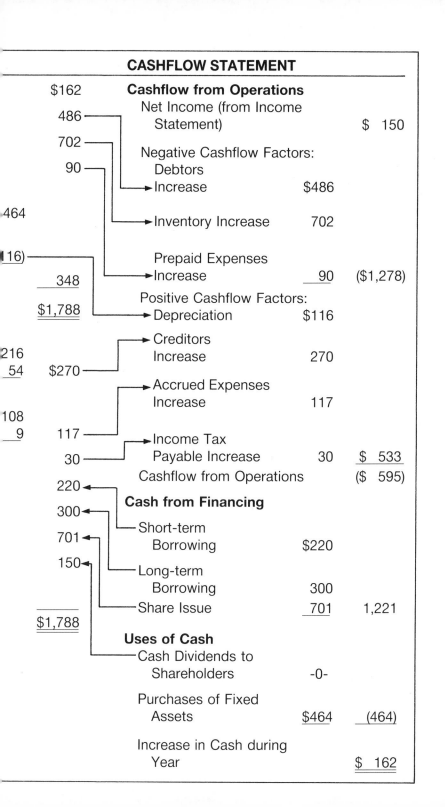

CASHFLOW STATEMENT

Cashflow from Operations

$162

486

702

90

464

(16)

348

$1,788

216

54   $270

108

9

117

30

220

300

701

150

$1,788

Net Income (from Income Statement)		$ 150
Negative Cashflow Factors: Debtors		
Increase	$486	
Inventory Increase	702	
Prepaid Expenses Increase	90	($1,278)
Positive Cashflow Factors: Depreciation	$116	
Creditors Increase	270	
Accrued Expenses Increase	117	
Income Tax Payable Increase	30	$ 533
Cashflow from Operations		($ 595)

Cash from Financing

Short-term Borrowing	$220	
Long-term Borrowing	300	
Share Issue	701	1,221

Uses of Cash

Cash Dividends to Shareholders	-0-	
Purchases of Fixed Assets	$464	(464)
Increase in Cash during Year		$ 162

been expended in the course of the period covered, to immediately generate those sales. It does not include assets that are purchased and that will produce income in the future, such as plant and equipment. Hence the difference between expenses or payments which appear in a profit and loss statement and payments which appear in the balance sheet. So that we are comparing apples with apples, we are comparing income generated in a particular period with expenses incurred and spent in earning that income.

The other document, the balance sheet, represents the actual net worth of the business, that is, what it is worth at a particular point in time. It is calculated by deducting liabilities from assets to arrive at the net worth of your equity (known as owner's equity, or sometimes called partnership's or shareholders' funds). The assets mentioned previously are assets which produce income; they can be plant and equipment, motor vehicles, land, anything which produces income for more than the period over which the statements have been prepared. Liabilities, on the other hand, obviously represent money you owe, to banks, creditors, finance companies and so on.

By comparing the status of assets and liabilities from month to month you can determine the financial performance of your business. The profit and loss statement shows the short-term profit or loss for a given period. The balance sheet represents the result of those profits and losses accumulated over a number of short periods to show the net position or net worth of the business. The cashflow statement, the profit and loss statement and the balance sheet, when read in conjunction with each other, give a total picture of the financial status of your business.

The three financial statements shown on pages 154–5 relate to the first year of trading of a small manufacturing business. The important connections are shown by arrows. Reading these connections is a little like looking at a chessboard in the middle of a game. Each piece must be studied in relation to the other pieces so that an overall pattern and situation can be gleaned. A detailed analysis of these relationships is given in the Appendix, on pages 234–9.

When it comes to reporting and bookkeeping it is a good idea to do things manually first, before rushing off to use a computer, so that you develop a basic understanding of how book records are to be kept and financial statements drawn up. Just as you should initially do your own production, your own selling, your own debt collection and so on, do your own bookkeeping under your accountant's guidance and you will get a feeling for how your business is going. Look at it on the paper in front of you, look at what you have actually spent versus what you have actually earned.

Don't get too sophisticated. I've seen people who have orchards and grocery shops running the best accounting systems of all. They know exactly how much things cost them each day. Grocers know exactly what their costs are at the market, exactly what they have to charge for apples and pears per kilogram to make a profit. They know that they have to sell things at a certain price to make a profit. They also know what their shop is costing them, how much rent they are paying, what their fixed costs are. They don't use computers, but they are making a profit.

A very important report for every small business owner is the one-page summary. This should be prepared at the end of every week or at least at the end of the month. It summarises all the reports and relevant figures which have already been mentioned. The one-page summary sets out your financial position, your performance, in terms of:

- sales for the period,
- purchases for the period,
- expenses for the period,
- net profit for the period, and
- break-even point.

It also gives a picture of your financial health — stock level and debtors versus bank overdraft and creditors — to ascertain your liquidity level.

Make your one-page summary in your diary. You should look at it daily, compare it with last month/last year, constantly read it and pore over it, to get a real and accurate knowledge of how you are doing. Here is a sample:

The One-page Summary

SALES			PURCHASES	
Division	$			$
Division	$			
			OVERHEAD EXPENSES	
			Selling	$
			Administration	$
			FINANCE	
			Interest	$
		————		————
SUB TOTAL	$ ————		SUB TOTAL	$ ————
NET PROFIT (LOSS)	$ ————			

ASSETS			LIABILITIES	
BANK	$		BANK OVERDRAFT	$
DEBTORS TOTAL			CREDITORS TOTAL	
30	$		30	$
60	$		60	$
> 90	$		> 90	$
Stock	$			
	————			————
SUB TOTAL	$ ————		SUB TOTAL	$ ————
NET WORKING CAPITAL	$ ————			
FIXED ASSETS			LOANS	
Plant	$		Leases	$
Land	$		Hire purchase	
	————			————
SUB TOTAL	$ ————		SUB TOTAL	$ ————
NET WORTH	$ ————			

This suggested format allows you to compare your weekly/monthly profits/loss performance. It enables you to compare your current assets with current liabilities to determine your cash liquidity position. It breaks down debtors to see whether any problems exist in payment to you, and creditors to show whether you are having any difficulties, and to what extent. It also reviews your long-term assets versus liabilities to arrive at your net financial position. In my experience the business operator who uses a one-page summary is always successful.

MEETINGS — WHO NEEDS THEM?

The typical enterpriser often finds meetings a bore. But meetings are an inevitable and important part of business life, be they with the bank manager, with creditors, with customers or with your own directors, boards of management and employees. My favourite sort of meeting is held in a restaurant (for breakfast, lunch or dinner). Meeting over a meal is better suited to small numbers (ideally two) and is friendlier and less formal. If you are the host, you will have the advantage that your guest(s) will usually be more vulnerable and receptive. However, these sorts of meetings are better for marketing than for matters requiring a less distracting environment.

Meetings should be run properly, at a fixed time and to a strict agenda. Minutes of the previous meeting, even reports that are to be tabled, should have been circulated as early as possible before the meeting. Everybody should turn up on time and the meeting should begin as scheduled. The meeting shouldn't go for hours because people's attention span simply doesn't last that long. The meeting should commence with recording or reviewing the previous minutes and what action has been taken as a result.

Directors' meetings with your external director/mentor in attendance (and your accountant invited when appropriate) should be held monthly. The agenda suited to your business will follow the headings in your business plan and will address general matters discussed in this book — cashflow, bureaucratic regulations, and so on. Meetings to do with more detailed matters such as marketing, staff and business hardware should be held weekly at a time and place that does not interfere with the running of the business, preferably early in the morning when everyone is fresh and keen to get to the point.

If meetings achieve their purpose they are not boring and are certainly not a waste of time. Meetings are a forum for communication. They can be used for brainstorming and for creativity, and it is a good idea to get away to a different place where the phone doesn't ring, thinking can take place freely and discussion can occur. Meetings also can be a venue for solving interpersonal problems in the workplace. They give people the chance to put everything honestly on the table.

If you are just starting out you need not have an elaborate board meeting, but you must sit down once a week with your mentor or spouse or someone close to see how you have gone for the week, to analyse your sales and your costs. As I have already said, meet with your accountant once a month. I know it costs money, but this simply means you must use the time effectively. Send your financial figures to him or her beforehand, listing what accounting services you require. If someone does your books for you, he or she should attend the meeting to help explain the figures.

If you have any doubts or there is something you don't understand, your mentor or external director should be available to answer your questions. They might also help to make sure you are doing the right thing — not spending too much money, working hard, not feeling sorry for yourself. Unless you have inordinate powers of self-discipline, you will need someone there to keep pushing you — someone you respect and will take notice of. I don't think we deal with ourselves efficiently unless we refer our concerns and activities to someone else. It is almost like going to the teacher and reporting on what you have done for that week. It can be quite painful and annoying and seems like a waste of time, but it is a good thing because it gives you the chance to look at yourself in the mirror, as it were. Unless you have the discipline of someone else to do it with, you probably won't do it at all.

TIME MANAGEMENT

The typical enterpriser has too much to do and too little time in which to do it. Most small business people work more than fifty hours a week, but without effective time management much of their activity may well be wasted, particularly when they are tired or under financial stress. They may be frittering away hours on trivial, insignificant or irrelevant activities, whilst leaving vital tasks undone.

Two things — time and energy — are available to everyone, but they are not always used to the same effect. Your utilisation of energy and time determines how effective you are in business. Learn to control your business rather than letting it control you. It really comes back to self-discipline.

The best way to find out how effectively you are using your time is simply to write down exactly what you are doing every fifteen minutes for a full twenty-four-hour period (allowing for sleep) over two weeks and reflect on it at the end of every day. You can go to as many time management classes and courses as you want to, you can lash out on tapes and videos, but this is by far the most effective method of improving the use of your own time.

Effective managers put urgent jobs before less pressing ones, or first things first. They rank duties according to importance, deciding, for instance, which is more urgent — planning a new advertising campaign or hiring a new assistant. The best approach for tackling both routine duties and on-going projects is the preparation of daily, weekly and monthly time management schedules.

I prefer to plan for the week the Sunday before, going through my diary for each day. This process often reveals clashes. There are sometimes duplications of tasks and roles, and of meetings. You may find that re-scheduling will in fact increase productivity, not only for yourself but for your staff as well. In your planning you should allow times for emergencies and interruptions such as telephone calls. Indeed, depending on the sort of business you are in and how dependent you are on the telephone for communication, you might allocate times of the day when you make and receive all your telephone calls. Such systematic arrangement of tasks allows sufficient lead time for preparation of due-date material and all those disagreeable last-minute rushes.

Effective time management also means that your subordinates, particularly your secretary if you have one, can use their resources more efficiently. The owner/operator leads from the front; if you are an inefficient user of time, your whole operation will tend to be inefficient.

Part of the process of managing your time is managing your mind. Very often when you first start up a business your mind is highly active. It develops all sorts of ideas, it envisages problems, it works out solutions. This can happen at eight o'clock at night or at three in the morning. To unburden your brain you should write all these thoughts down. Your brain is a bit like a computer, in that it has a vast but limited capacity. Making a note of your thoughts is like freeing up the hard disk by copying data onto floppy disks: it creates space for more thinking. Don't worry about losing sleep; use the time wisely. If your brain wants to work let it work, if it doesn't want to work then let it rest. Furthermore, writing something down is a commitment. Once you have performed this physical act you have provided the momentum for taking action. The agony of facing a task on the list and the ecstasy that comes from crossing it off when it is done will give you the incentive to repeat the process, so write everything down and make sure you act on it. Don't re-prioritise your list and don't back out. If you have made a note to accomplish a task and you don't get to it, carry it forward to the next day in your diary.

Just as you plan for the full week on Sunday, organise for the next day at the end of the previous day. This will give you peace of mind at night, a feeling that you are on top of things, a real excitement about going to work the next morning. Simply by arranging the next day, defining on paper what you want to accomplish, you will feel you have a head start. Meanwhile your brain can begin working for you on the subconscious level. Also look back on the day just completed and review your accomplishments. List any matters which were not dealt with and must be carried forward.

Four basic steps to planning a day are:

1 Schedule time on your next day's page for appointments and meetings and consult your weekly and monthly calendar for details of what is ahead.

2 On a plain page schedule time for sleep and other leisure activities (for example, family activities).
3 Work on your activities page, assign priorities and schedule time on a planned page for, say, A-activities or B-activities. 'A' might be for business activities and you might prioritise them as 1A, 2A to 10A or however many activities you have. 'B' might be for leisure activities such as family, social, fitness, hobbies.
4 Invest at least ten minutes at the end of each day to record your achievements, record your expenses and to plan for the next day.

Planning ahead can include not only the week, but months and years — indeed, five years as per the business plan. It is all part of using your time efficiently to achieve your business (and personal) objectives. It is mostly a matter of maintaining control of your business by forcing activities into the time available rather than trying to expand the time to accommodate the activities. Many people fear that if they don't seem out of control they are not going to seem busy enough or important enough. They really don't want to manage their time well. Once you realise that controlling your time is not only more productive but more pleasant, the rest is fairly easy.

I hate leaving unfinished business or leaving anything hanging over my head and I work with great intensity to create moments of empty space — a minute, an hour or a weekend — in which to enjoy having nothing to do. These moments are the carrots at the end of the stick and by programming them into my schedule I force myself to finish the business activities leading up to them within the times specifically allocated. Such valuable 'free time' might allow for a problem to be solved or a new idea to arise.

An itinerary, a schedule or a task allocation is worthless unless you stick to it. A large part of sticking to your schedule is being aware that very few interruptions are so important that they have to be attended to immediately. Treat unexpected situations as you would any other time commitment. Don't respond immediately but programme time for dealing with them into your future schedule according to your priorities — that afternoon, tomorrow or next week, whenever you can fit them in. Sticking to a schedule is also made easier by allocating the appropriate amount of time to the activities that will fill it up. Don't try to do too much: you will end up frustrated by not doing anything properly.

Since most of the time in business we are dealing with people, we need to allow for personality. Everyone operates at a different pace. Some people are very quick on the telephone or in meetings and don't enter into much dialogue; whilst others, by their very nature, like to talk at length about the football and the weather or suchlike. Also, some people require more than one meeting, or protracted discussions and negotiations, in order to achieve objectives; whilst others, according to their personality or their circumstances or their place in the hierarchy, make decisions instantaneously. Try to learn as much as possible about the people you are dealing with, including employees. Get to understand their personalities and plan your time to accommodate them.

Often it is a good idea to do the things you least like doing at the beginning of the day to get them out of the way, or do quick tasks to build your sense of confidence and momentum for the rest of the day. Most small businesses have day-to-day problems of some sort (liquidity, dealing with banks, dealing with legal situations such as demand letters, and so forth), especially in hard times. Ideally you should allocate these to one or two times in the week, for an hour or so. This keeps the rest of the week free from thinking of, handling or even accepting phone calls about such odious, dreaded matters and allows you to concentrate fully on the productive, profitable side of the business — your marketing, quality control and cashflow. Using your diary or the day's activity planner, schedule these a week in advance, then you won't neglect them and you will be more efficient in handling them. Equally importantly, you won't be tempted to prioritise something else ahead of them.

The whole solution to mastering time is to do the things you planned to do when you planned on doing them and within the time you allocated for them.

A useful aid to time management is a very efficient filing system, one that suits you. So much time can be wasted trying to find a letter, a report or a note, not to mention personal paperwork, such as your will and all your household bills. Include in the filing system notes of all your conversations, no matter how brief, no matter how seemingly trivial. Learn by the example of your bank manager and lawyer. File all records of conversations under the client name or by subject, whichever makes more sense in your business. This will enable you readily to recall the conversation in the near or distant future, or to produce documentary evidence in the event of a dispute or an allegation. It could even mean the difference between losing or winning a court battle.

A critical aspect of time management is delegation — the process of assigning appropriate chores to subordinates so that you are freed up from routine operations. Failure or inability to delegate often entangles the small business owner in every-day activities at the expense of important ones such as planning or marketing and collecting cash. Symptoms of failure to delegate are obvious: the small business owner who is too hurried to be effective; the owner who makes costly mistakes in dealing with customers and staff; staff inability to take over in emergencies when the boss is ill or absent.

Autocratic or perfectionist small business owners rationalise their reluctance to delegate by insisting that no one can do the work as well as they. Ask yourself whether this is really the case. Surely there are some tasks that can be delegated to subordinates or lower paid employees. Proper training is the obvious foil for this obstacle. Make certain your subordinates understand their responsibilities, the limits of their authority and the results expected of them before they are turned loose on the task. Discuss their errors and show them ways of profiting from their mistakes.

Management experts stress one golden rule for successful delegation: take on the jobs you dislike or are not familiar with and delegate the ones you know and love. Managers who perform favoured tasks and pass on distasteful chores fail to acquire new knowledge that can help their companies' future

165

profits and succeed in losing the esteem of their staff. If you find it simply impossible to delegate, for whatever personal reason, then it is very important to recognise this weakness and at least employ others who can do what you don't want to do yourself. This should form part of the strengths and weaknesses analysis you do right at the beginning, in your business plan.

THE BURDEN OF BUREAUCRACY

One of the major operating costs to business is government red tape. Form completion and compliance with myriad regulations places a heavy burden on the small operator's time at the expense of productive business activity. The only way to cope with this is to be aware of the regulations and dutifully comply with them, even if you don't understand them and have scant regard for them. Consult your accountant if necessary.

I do not intend to go into detail here about the various regulations that apply to small business (they warrant a book in themselves). Rather, let it suffice to mention some of the regulatory bodies to which enterprisers are commonly beholden.

The Australian Taxation Office administers sales tax, income tax, company tax, fringe benefits tax, withholding tax and prescribed payment tax. The Australian Bureau of Statistics from time to time requires detailed statistical information.

The State Government enforces labour regulations, such as payroll tax, health department regulations and regulations under the Accident Compensation Commission, to name but a few. It also administers capital gains tax.

Then there are consumer laws. Now that consumer protection is an entrenched feature of Australian business, every trader who engages in a consumer transaction needs to have a good idea of what consumer protection involves. In order to avoid inadvertent breaches of these laws the small business operator needs to know about consumers' and traders' rights in any dispute. The most significant aspect of this legislation is the Trade Practices Act which applies nationally and covers advertising, promotion, and so on.

A vast range of registrations is also required for some businesses, for hospitals and for accommodation homes. These apply to names, patents and corporate structures. Licensing is required for certain premises, food, restaurants, lifts and cranes, professions, tradespeople, solicitors, estate agents, medical practitioners, and so on. Permits are required for certain business activities, poisons, scaffolding, the transportation of food, and hawking. Regulation of business activities includes consumer sales, advertising, record keeping, labelling. Compulsory insurances also apply to third party vehicles and workers' compensation. There is also registration of business for sales tax, registration of employees, registration of premises, and so on. There are liquor licences, newsagency agreements, other guard agency agreements and second-hand dealers' licences. It might be a good idea to pay your accountant to prepare the documentation if any of these regulations affects you, provided you obtain a quote. Given the penalties for non-compliance, this might be cheaper than attempting to go it alone.

Finally, be alert to the complicated and ever-changing superannuation productivity area. You should consult an adviser on this.

MARKETING AND SALES

We saw earlier that the first ingredient for success is to make a sale. But sales don't happen automatically. You must find, woo and win your market. This is hard enough in good times; but in tough times the enterpriser has to work harder, smarter and longer to achieve it.

I can imagine your objections at this point: 'Marketing! We need to sell more products, earn more money, survive. The marketing's obvious.' And so it may seem. But amongst the confusion and pressures of small business, particularly in hard times, it is vital to be disciplined and to know where you are going. A similar concept applies to the defence forces, where young recruits are drilled in polishing their boots and making their beds in a certain way. Why? Does this make them better fighters? Not directly, but it is a discipline. If they perfect self-discipline they will study and train better, they will prepare their equipment more efficiently; therefore making their beds and polishing their boots every morning and night will, indirectly, make them better fighters. Likewise, the marketing plan that we discussed in chapter 3 is a form of discipline. It forces you to set schedules and expense budgets. It tells all those around you exactly what is required of them and when.

The rationale behind marketing is really very stark: no matter how brilliant your service or product or how cost effective or cost saving you can be to others, the phone will not ring unless you tell people about it. Once they are aware you must then ensure that you can satisfy their needs profitably. Ways of alerting your potential clients to your product or service are many and spectacularly varied. They include: print media, advertising editorial, radio, television, brochures, letter box drops, direct mail, lecture circuits, personal selling, word-of-mouth support, social and club contacts, posters and signage, and so on. Publications exist which can guide you in choosing the most appropriate means for your business (see Bibliography, page 240).

Using the business plan outlined in chapter 3, you will have established the marketing edge of your product or service and researched your competition. From the marketing plan built around that research you will have a clear picture of your objectives, where you are going to position your product, the target market you are after, your range, your pricing and trading strategy, the logistics of delivery, administration, your required sales force, the advertising, promotion and public relations you are going to use, the resources you require, and finally your budgets and targets.

Strict adherence to sales budgets becomes even more important than usual in tough times, as it will generate the profits that enable you to pay your overheads and your own wage. Sales budgets should clearly itemise each of the main costs, and where and when staff should be employed and trained. They should also break down your products and services into different segments.

If you have sales staff let them know what marketing you are undertaking and what expenditure you are incurring, ask for their opinion, show real and obvious concern for them. They are far more important than a computer print-out. Delegate to them as much responsibility as possible. Use the budget and sales forecast to deepen your understanding, not as an exercise in accounting practice. Make the budget interesting and easy to use. Change and re-draft the whole budget if it proves to be wrong and limiting. A sales budget will be valuable only if it produces information which is relevant, timely, easy to assimilate and easy to understand. It must be produced quickly, in time to be of the most use, with a high degree of detail, and as concisely as possible. Above all it must be usable by the people who are to benefit from it.

Keep your plan tight and to the point. Short, sharp statements should be included. For example, a statement under your context heading might be as follows: 'Marketing objectives to ensure existing clients know that our company is the best in its field.'

In hard times concentrate on face-to-face marketing. Be at the coal face, be in front of your customers, go to their offices, see how they operate their factories, understand how they think. The best way you can market yourself to them, no matter what you are trying to sell, is to get to know them, make them your friends. One way to do this is to have a card on every client or every chief executive or purchasing officer of the client you are dealing with. Record personal details — quirks, interests, sport, musical tastes, and so on. Also understand your client's business so that you can offer alternatives that are acceptable. Understand your client's seasonal peaks and troughs, stock and stock control generally. Understand how they earn their profits and assist you in trading term flexibility or otherwise. (I believe customers who earn cash — for example, take-away food outlets — should pay cash.) Generally people like to know that someone cares about them, socially and professionally. It is nice to receive a birthday or anniversary card and congratulations when your particular team wins. You must service, service and service your customers in every acceptable way imaginable, without going over the top. I don't believe in relying on mail; I think the direct approach is preferable to the lazier third-party style of marketing, such as advertising, though it has a place in certain circumstances.

The cheapest marketing data base is made up of leads and referrals from existing satisfied customers, not an expensive mailing list or advertising in glossy national magazines. It is one on one, it is being where your customer is. Find out through your own market research where your customer is and be there, bump into them. Be at the social occasions, get their business card and then choose how, when and where you wish to contact them. If you are constantly found where your customers are, they will start to think, Well, he/she isn't a bad sort of person, he/she is doing all right, he/she is in my sphere of activity.

The formula for successful marketing is therefore footwork, friendship and trust. What do the insurance companies often do when people first join them? They get them to go and sell to all their friends and family, their loved ones. Just like your accountant and your bank manager, a customer faced with ten phone messages on their desk is obviously more likely to ring you first if you are a friend. This certainly makes life more enjoyable and it has the added financial reward that your customers are going to prefer to deal with you, regardless of the comparative merits of your product or service.

One method of cutting back marketing costs is to target and direct-market your customers. This must then be followed up with written materials. Keep in constant contact with your clients. You will get the order if you are there at the time.

CASE STUDY:

An acquaintance of mine is in the computer business and sells mainframe computers. He is dealing mainly with large corporations or government bureaucracies and his orders range from $2000 to $20m. He will spend months and months and occasionally years just building up a relationship before the person has even identified the need to buy a computer. He is just developing a relationship with a view to making a sale; and he usually reaches his target. In some cases, of course, the company is taken over before he achieves his aim; but that is the risk he has to take.

The way in which your telephone is answered gives your clients a window onto your business. A bright, cheery, helpful receptionist will do more for your marketing than you will fully appreciate. We all know that it makes you feel good to deal with a firm when you are on hold for only a short period of time and yet the receptionist keeps coming back to you. There is nothing worse than being on hold for an eternity and being assaulted with muzak or an irritating radio station. The physical make-up of your reception area is also important, and you might like to adorn it with flowers, magazines, or even sweets for your customers.

Don't over-estimate the marketing potential of trade exhibitions or conventions. Recently I went to an accounting convention. It was impossible not to notice the healthy supply of computer software, investment opportunities and accounting services, but one very small booth that stood out even more was occupied by a company selling leather products — diaries, and so on. They attracted the most interest. Perhaps the investment advisers and computer people would have been better off marketing their product at something totally unrelated, such as a food exhibition, where they would have been more noticeable.

If you decide to use advertising as one of your marketing tools, be sure to get a return on your advertising investment dollar. Use your dollar strategically and monitor and measure its effectiveness. There are no hard and fast rules as to how much you should spend. Each organisation varies. Some allow a proportion of the sales that are expected to result.

But before contemplating advertising of any kind, establish who you are trying to attract and what you wish to achieve. Advertising starts at your front door. Carefully study your existing customers and if possible introduce new products to them. Request introductions to other divisions and/or subsidiaries. Even try for introductions to your customers' clients. It is the most effective and most immediate placement of your advertising and marketing resources. Once these avenues have been exhausted establish who you are going to attract to buy from your company. Approach the market with a clear picture of what you hope to achieve.

CASE STUDY:

A friend of mine has a hotel with the best restaurant in the area. She was always overbooked on Thursdays, Fridays and Saturdays but rarely had bookings on Mondays or Tuesdays. She commenced an advertising campaign aimed at the type of people who frequented her restaurant from Thursday to Saturday. She advertised in the State print media and spent ten times her advertising budget with absolutely no sign of increased sales.

Her mistake was that she didn't aim her advertising strategically. It was commonsense that if existing clients rarely ate out on Mondays and Tuesdays why should similar types of clients from a wider area be any different? I suggested to her that she target a particular group and endeavour to attract them by making a series of special offers. These included a free meal for any aged pensioner having lunch with a paying customer. This was designed to entice the existing clientele to bring their parents. Also, any group of six or more would get a twenty-five per cent discount. Budget-conscious pensioners started enjoying the restaurant on Mondays and Tuesdays almost immediately. My friend also employed a home-care nurse to assist parents with their children when they came to lunch or dinner on a Monday or Tuesday. The advertising was inexpensive and very effective. It consisted of a local suburban newspaper advertisement and notices sent to local clubs and baby health centres.

When it comes to selling I believe in what is the called the ABC Customer Selection process. The most profitable clients are classified under category A, and are serviced very efficiently and given the most attention. Clients in a sort of limbo, who will either ripen to A grade clients or will eventually be placed in C grade, are classified under category B, and are visited and supported slightly less than the A clients. The C category customer may receive a visit or telephone call from the company once or twice a year but their needs are serviced by internal sales staff or by a sales representative who is sent to them to explore opportunities or problems as they arise.

If employing sales staff, don't confuse the role of a sales professional with that of an order taker. The former should be distinguished by certain qualities, the first of which is courage. It certainly takes courage to earn one's income purely from commission or brokerage. Secondly, sales professionals must have detailed knowledge of their market and of their customers. Thirdly, they must be able to position themselves as specialists. Generally a market segment can be penetrated more rapidly and more deeply by concentrated fire power. Another unique characteristic is that they will have shown an ability to succeed in their target market segment — for example, manufacturing. Most sales professionals also manage to glean information from the most unusual sources to become fully informed. As a consequence of their research and target marketing, they become recognised experts in their field. Customers will come to them rather than their needing to seek out customers. They will gain a reputation around the marketplace. If you place a sales professional in a purely order-taking role you are depriving him or her of opportunities to use the above skills. Conversely, if you place an order taker in a selling role you could cause stress leading to fear and inferiority complexes, and certainly no sales will be made.

I believe that ninety per cent of an order clerk's salary should be in the form of guaranteed pay and ten per cent should be based on performance. By contrast, a sales professional should receive no more than twenty per cent as a retainer and eighty per cent in incentives. In these hard times you might try asking your sales people to contribute to overheads in exchange for one hundred per cent commission. It is one way to cut down any costs while you are building scope to increase your sales. Sales professionals should have no upper limit to their earning potential. I see no problem with the sales professional earning a lot more than the owner of the company.

Whatever sales system you adopt it is important that staff report to the manager or yourself weekly and fill out detailed reports — who they visited, what was said, the required follow-up. You should review these every week and compare them with the previous week's. Ensure that every product being sold is at the standard gross or net profit margin. It is profit that keeps the business going, not turnover. Some sales professionals are quite cunning about producing the turnover but profit is hard to find. Ensure that your sales staff sell only to approved customers. Pay your commissions monthly; don't get behind — it is the quickest way to destroy staff morale. Run regular internal competitions to add variety to the competitive spirit. For example, any sales professional introducing five new clients in a month could receive a dinner for two with accommodation at a local five-star hotel. These should be built into your budget and only claimable once the profit has been achieved.

Most sales professionals will have their own system of control and recording, but it is very important that they share their system with you because it is basically your customer and your product and you need to know the mechanics of how your customer is being serviced. It is important to make sure that they keep a diary and manage their time efficiently. They should be pro-active, rather than reactive, to the customer's requirements. Card systems must be maintained in duplicate so that the internal sales team have a record of recent promises, discounts, deals or special arrangements with clients. I believe that the sales professional's success should be judged in terms of the journey, not the destination. Because of this I feel that he or she should constantly be moved on to new areas that need developing. Financial consideration can be provided during this changeover period.

Sales professionals should be fully acquainted with their

customers and their customers' financial position, not only so that they can sell more effectively but so that you will be confident of getting paid. Particularly in a tough economic environment, it is important to sell but not to push too hard. Many a time, customer resistance is based on the knowledge that they cannot buy because they cannot afford to pay. And remember, there's no point in making a sale if you can't collect.

CASE STUDY:

A client of mine is in the clothing manufacturing business, supplying mainly to retailers. He faces stiff competition and he is vulnerable to the possibility of his customers going down the tube. He has hit on a new idea to do with the value-added concept. He offers a free computer service which analyses the vital accounting and bookkeeping statistics of his customers' businesses. He sends these customers a questionnaire which they complete on a monthly basis, giving their vital sales figures, purchasing costs, lines they are carrying, turnover, number of customers, and so on. They also include their budgets. My client gets all this information, compiles and consolidates it and then shoots back an analysis of how that customer is going compared to the other users of the system (anonymously, of course). The benefit is that he is helping his customers improve their profits and their business management. Generally, people who are taking advantage of this service are interested in being more profitable anyway. So, in locking his customers in to his service, he is helping them to become more profitable and because of this they are in turn able to purchase more of his products. It is also a means of monitoring how his customers are going. In these tough economic times he can identify which of his customers are getting into financial trouble. He can offer ways to help them and even then, if it looks like they are going to get into financial trouble, he can withdraw from them in advance of copping a bad debt.

Finally, make sure your sales professionals are able to:

- ask for the order;
- earn loyalty by empathising with the customer at all times;
- ensure their facts are correct, not only about your business but about their clients;
- know the correct title and position of the client they are dealing with, and try to reach the decision maker as quickly as possible and approach them properly;
- always show that they care about their client's business as well as their own. Try to judge the people they are selling to — are they aggressive, timid, apprehensive, and so on — and act accordingly;
- develop the skill of listening;
- always fulfil promises, follow up, document what they say they will do and do it on time, telling the client in advance if they are unable to do it;
- adopt good time management techniques;
- adopt the KIS (Keep It Simple) principle;
- be efficient and keep tidy work areas;
- attend to the following:

   — Appearance: Look and feel comfortable. Wear the right clothes. Be groomed accordingly. Drive a reliable vehicle that suits your position.

   — Equipment: Always have handy a spare pen and paper, a wristwatch that is accurate and some change for a telephone call or the parking meter.

   — Card system: An efficient card system or computer diary is vital. The card system should be clear, up to date and full of facts about the client, containing at least twenty pieces of information for each contact.

   — Diary: A diary is the heart of a good salesperson's hardware and should be used throughout a busy and varied day to make notes for later review

176

and transferral to the card system or a note book. Action notes should also be made in the diary for follow-up.

DIVERSIFICATION — THE RISKS

With the freedom of running your own business comes the inevitable temptation to spread into new areas of endeavour. This is particularly the case for creative people, people with active, restless minds — people with the very enterprising traits that led them into their own business in the first place. But diversification can be a mistake: you might be better off sticking to what you know, the area in which you have experience, contacts and technical know-how — or, as the jargon goes, 'sticking to the knitting'. Part of the reason for having a mentor or an independent strategic planner on your board of directors is in fact to help you 'stick to the knitting'.

Resisting the urge to diversify often means persisting with a business activity which is downright boring. However, as I have said, boredom often equates to cashflow, which equates to profits. It is common to see a business which is successful in one capital city expand into other States for the sake of it. But this duplicates overheads, communication costs, travel costs and accommodation costs. It doesn't help in the overall objective of achieving profits. It is also common to see enterprisers make a lot of money out of property speculation and, suddenly thinking they are the greatest business managers on earth, they move into manufacturing or some other area of business in which they have no expertise at all.

CASE STUDY:

Darren worked in the hardware industry in Sydney. His business was basically driven by him. He worked very hard but didn't pay much attention to monthly figures, margins and collecting his money. It was left to his wife to

---

sort out the books and get things in order from time to time. After some years, Darren got itchy feet and went for a trip to Brisbane. There he discovered a warmer climate and, claiming that this meant a greater demand for his product and his marketing expertise, he proceeded to set up an interstate office. He travelled frequently between Sydney and Brisbane on the pretext of keeping an eye on the business, but failed to spend time with his staff there because he was in fact more interested in his new social life. The business lost money from the start.

We had a chat with Darren, and eventually he decided to close the interstate office and stop the rot. But he was unable to sub-let the premises, so his $5000 loss per month, although less than an initial $20,000, was still a substantial amount for a small business.

Of course, you must occasionally take stock of the environment in which you operate and this might suggest the desirability of moving into a different line. But, rather than stray from your company's known strengths, you should look at making greater use of them in a different way.

You may identify the need for a new product or service to market to your current customers, or for developing a new market for existing products. New fields may open themselves to you through the acquisition of other concerns or the purchasing of manufacturing licences. If this is the case, take a close look at your resources, your property, your own skills and your strengths and weaknesses. What plant, labour, finance do you have available? Are they being utilised to their most profitable extent? Analyse sales patterns and estimate demand, both short and long term.

Research other possibilities. Beware of entering any high-technology market when introducing a new product. It is safer to rely on bread-and-butter lines unless you are fortunate enough to have the necessary technical expertise in-house. Again, aim at staying within the boundaries of your business's established strengths and the industry you know.

However, there are circumstances under which a business can diversify successfully. The most common opportunities are when profit or growth objectives cannot be achieved through the existing business, when the existing business is too dependent on one industry, market or customer, when cashflow exceeds current requirements, when competition is depressing growth of profit margins, or when major customers decide to make the product themselves. It is certainly crucial to diversify your customer base, so that your financial viability is not dependent on anyone else's.

If you have decided to diversify for any of the above reasons, you must be prepared to raise large sums of money and, if necessary, to locate suitable ventures. This involves a disciplined and far-reaching search for opportunities and includes surveys of past growth markets, new technologies, large or larger markets, firms of potential that are badly managed, profitable companies with a similar major shareholder, and existing synergy. (Synergy comes in various forms: sales synergy, in which products have common distribution outlets, administration, warehousing or advertising; operating synergy, in which manufacturing plants can be combined to reduce overheads; and research and development synergy.)

Under appropriate circumstances diversification can bring major benefits to small businesses by reducing dependency on a particular market, by equalising sales in cyclical markets or by offering opportunities in growth markets. The first step is to prepare a new or an amended business plan. But be warned: diversification is risky.

HANDLING SUCCESS

Contrary to popular mythology, success in business brings its own set of problems and therefore requires careful management. Whereas sudden failure has a sobering effect, sudden success is inclined to give business operators a false sense of security. Yet, as we said at the outset, it is an absolute certainty that bad times will follow good (how quickly, we don't know) and a flush period should be used to prepare for an inevitable period of stringency.

Proper financial planning will take the guesswork out of reading the commercial wheel of fortune. By keeping you in touch with the exact current status of your business, it will enable you to make accurate predictions about the immediate future and give you a broad picture of the longer term. Ideally, it will prepare you for any eventuality, positive or negative, and will enable you to anticipate rises and falls in cashflow.

When the good times do roll, the enterpriser's attitude is important. Don't let success go to your head. Don't get carried away with your own grandeur. Continue to work for tomorrow, not for today. Persist with the hard jobs. Continue to lead by example. Don't employ excess staff or purchase or lease expensive equipment for the sake of it. Don't go out and squander your wealth on expensive cars or overseas holidays on the pretext of a tax deduction. The debt will still be there when the cashflow has long since dried up. Remember the fundamental rule: do what is best for yourself and your family first; then consider cashflow (even in good times); and last of all consider what is best for tax. Stick to your business plan and listen to your advisers. So many business people from humble beginnings lose their sense of perspective at the first sign of substantial profits. They change their lifestyles dramatically, they neglect their businesses and they very quickly go to the wall. Don't be like them; be an enterpriser not an entrepreneur.

Build soundly and don't manipulate. Don't assume that if you succeed in one business area or product you will automatically succeed in another. By all means diversify your cashflows, but do it carefully.

Stick to your budgets, every line of them. Always compare with the actual expenditures, particularly those in the personal area of travel, entertainment, cash. Use profits gained in good times to provide for the not-so-good times or unforeseen disasters, or for expansion. The fundamental rule of putting aside ten per cent of your profit as spare cash for emergencies or company expansion is a good one. If you develop this habit during easy times it will be firmly entrenched when things get difficult. Now is the time to make sound investments, but be sure to diversify them and maintain flexibility so that you can grow carefully and gently. Spread your investments amongst the various sectors — property, cash, shares, bonds and so on — and ensure that each investment has a separate legal owner, all controlled by your family.

Now is also the time to improve your people skills through courses and seminars and to invest in staff training. Having built up the marketing and/or production side of the business you should now concentrate on recruiting, managing, motivating and retaining valued staff. People are the most important aspect of your growth. Practise delegation. Many businesses eventually fail or do not achieve their full potential because of their founder's inability to delegate and manage people. Use the luxury of financial stability to transfer some of the load onto your staff; if this causes hiccups you will have the resources to cover them. Delegation is too late when tough times have already set in.

Continually reassess your own strengths and weaknesses and, as your business grows, the strengths and weaknesses of your business. Diversify into other areas only if they capitalise on your strengths and overcome your weaknesses.

The more successful your business becomes, the more you should review and rewrite your business plan, and the greater the attention you should pay to the fundamentals of setting personal financial goals and personal financial planning (refer to my book *Your Money and Your Life*, Lothian, 1989), analysing your current financial position and your borrowing, retirement planning, training, good advice, budgeting and reporting, time management and tax planning. In business you must always expect the tide to turn; you must always plan for tomorrow by setting aside cash reserves and lines of credit.

PART THREE: STAYING THERE

CHAPTER 7

Protecting Yourself and Your Business

As we have seen, most of the hard work in the life of a small business is devoted to *getting there* and to the managerial art of *being there*. The vital, and — in tough times — precarious, issue of *staying there* depends largely on protecting what has been achieved, personally as well as professionally.

LOOKING AFTER YOURSELF

We all know the theories about working for yourself: you have more free time, you are your own boss, you have flexible hours, you have time to look after yourself. But how often is this really the case? There is an opportunity perhaps for some improved quality of life. You may be able to live closer to your work, free of frustrating parking problems; you might get greater satisfaction from being a part of the enterprise for which you work. On the other hand, self-employment is also riskier, as we all know. It has been reported that between twenty and thirty per cent of business executives die before the age of sixty, and Australia has seen its fair share of such tragedies recently. The greatest hazards include the illusion of indispensability, spouse pressure, not being able to lock the problems behind the office door at night, not taking a proper holiday, and lack of attention to exercise and diet. These can lead to ill-health, an early death or interpersonal problems. Tough economic times, in particular, take their toll on self-employed people.

All the above hazards can be minimised, if not eliminated, by time management and planning. Just as your business itself benefits from having a basic purpose, long- and short-term objectives and adequate resources, so will you personally. People who plan their lives automatically take into consideration their personal resources, capabilities, preferences and limitations, and are therefore able to recognise and seize opportunities as they come along.

It is just as important to know what manner of person has a disease as to know what disease the person has. In other words, mental and physical health are interdependent. We cannot eliminate worry altogether, but when we are well and rested the worry assumes its true proportions instead of being magnified. Likewise, the right mental attitude contributes to good physical health, which postpones the onset of old age, and this in turn enables us to cope much more easily with business problems.

In recent years much has been said and written about the health of business executives and the stress of modern business life. But it all boils down to the application of day-to-day commonsense. Intelligent living habits do much to ensure the smooth functioning of your system. Food, rest and exercise should be regulated and balanced — all things in moderation. Try to stay within ten per cent of your ideal body weight. Exercise is important for keeping toned and for relaxing, as well as for stimulating creative thought. Above all, maintain a positive attitude. It is easier said than done, but warding off depression is an important weapon against failure in adverse circumstances. Seek professional help if you feel unable to cope with the problems yourself.

Also look after yourself materially. You should allow yourself enough money to maintain an appropriate standard of living and to guard against risks. Do a personal budget along the lines of your business budget, allowing for all your expenses and your holidays. Attend to all aspects of your personal financial planning — identify personal goals and objectives and plan your investments, borrowings and budgeting, make sure you have more money coming in than going out. Bring your will up to date, plan for retirement, make sure you have adequate insurance against illness, against loss of income and against death.

If you have dependants make sure there is more than enough money to provide for them in the unfortunate event of your death. Allow for the payment of all bills and ensure that there is sufficient money to maintain the family's lifestyle and the children's education requirements where applicable.

Above all, enjoy what you do for a living. At least a third of your life is spent at work. If it doesn't give you happiness and satisfaction, the other two-thirds are not much good to you.

LOOKING AFTER YOUR BUSINESS

To many people, insurance is nothing more than a dirty word and a waste of money. An individual may well get away with such a cavalier attitude, but in business the range of potential disasters is so vast that insurance makes more sense than ever before. And in tough times the probability that those potential disasters will actually happen increases so significantly that a failure to insure against them is equivalent to financial suicide.

If you did not do so when first setting up, you should think seriously about covering your business for the following major contingencies: theft or damage of contents, including theft of cash; public, and possibly private, liability; professional liability; workers' compensation; loss of profit; damage to vehicles, premises, private cars, goods and so forth; debtors' failure to pay; and possibly most important of all, your own disability.

Before looking into the details of different insurance covers, you should identify the risks you face by carrying out a 'risk audit'. This involves a complete analysis of your business to see what dangers exist and what you can do about them. Obviously it is much better, wherever possible, to avoid risk by prevention. This can be done simply by being more careful, attending to dangerous equipment and slippery surfaces, making sure your staff are educated in safety regulations and procedures, and making sure they look after themselves. Make sure your premises have all appropriate fire safety equipment — extinguishers (for paper and electrical fires), first aid kits, burglar alarms. Make sure tools and sharp objects are stored neatly and safely when not in use and that waste is removed regularly. Promptly repair any faults to buildings, equipment, motor vehicles, plumbing facilities and electrical systems. All work should be carried out by qualified tradespeople.

If you have recently joined the ranks of the self-employed your personal insurance position will warrant review. No longer is an employer in the wings waiting to pay your superannuation or a pension. When considering your own needs don't forget your spouse and children if you are married. Family income benefits are not normally very expensive to set up and would make a huge difference to those left behind in the event of a calamity. You should think seriously about arranging cover on your directors' and partners' lives for the benefit of the business in the event of their early demise.

Additionally, you should have an ordinary Life policy, preferably of the endowment type. This is one that pays out after a set number of years or in the event of death. If this is too expensive to maintain initially, take out a term cover, which you will be able to convert into a Whole of Life policy when cashflow permits. Finally, consider the benefits of private health insurance, the premiums of which are usually fairly modest.

Obviously fire cover should be considered, to protect principal assets and consequential loss of profits. There is also public liability to cover your liability to third parties for personal injury or property damage. There is the employer's liability under the Accident Compensation Act (WorkCare in Victoria). And a number of other policies might be appropriate, depending on the type of industry you are in. These include: contractor's risk, boiler explosion, plate glass, product liability, marine transit, personal accident and illness, electronic equipment, machinery breakdown, and 'fidelity guaranteed' to protect you against employees embezzling or stealing goods or money. In line with modern business practices some insurers now offer package policies — for example, industrial, office or farm packs.

You should be careful to read all your policy documents very carefully to see what has been deleted and what is excluded, particularly when it comes to storm and tempest, rainwater damage, and flood.

Also beware of the danger of under-insurance. Under the terms of the 'co-insurance' clause, the insurance company will cover you only for the proportion of the total by which you are insured. This works as follows: if a person in a business insures goods worth $100,000 for only $50,000, and the entire stock is destroyed, $50,000 will be paid out and the business will lose out by $50,000. However, if only half the stock insured for $50,000 was destroyed, the insurance company would pay only $25,000. The rationale is that the destructive force — fire, and so on — would not have been so selective as to have destroyed only the insured stock. The most common co-insurance ratio — that is, the proportion of total cover that the insurance company will pay out regardless of your actual cover, is ninety per cent. This is quite generous, but there is no law saying that it has to be so.

Don't skimp on insurance. Deal only with first-class brokers or insurance companies with a good reputation for prompt payment of claims. You should actively manage your insurances and not let any policies lapse. It is most advantageous to review all your insurances at the same time, on an annual basis, if not six-monthly.

THE LAW: FOR AND AGAINST YOU

The law as it affects small business is complicated and detailed, and beyond the scope of this book. The law exists to protect you, but your own ignorance can make it work against you. With the help of your chosen solicitor or solicitors, you should inform yourself of the ins and outs of some or all of the following as they become relevant: statute law, common law, contract law, consumer protection under the Trades Practices Act, copyright designs, trademarks and trade names acts and laws, employer and employee laws, contracts of employment, leases, rent and hire purchase, the various companies Acts and Codes, Stock Exchange requirements, regulations to do with businesses and to do with use of premises, to do with local councils, State departments of labour, industry and so on, registrations, permits, licences or agencies, health requirements and electrical installation requirements.

You must take personal responsibility for reading all legal documentation pertaining to your business. There are no safe shortcuts or compromises. I know the fine print is boring and hard to understand, but you must tackle it so that no one else can be blamed for any misrepresentation. You must read legal documentation very carefully, even when you are signing a lease. Be aware that most legal documents to do with renting, leasing, hire purchasing, buying or borrowing have personal guarantees in them. The personal guarantee, as discussed earlier, is the very shirt off your back and, wherever possible, you should avoid signing one. If there is no option, make sure that your liability is limited to a specific amount or to a specific facility and that any multiple guarantees are 'several' rather than 'joint and several'. (The former means that any one party is liable only for his or her portion of the debt. The latter means that any one party can be held liable for the total debt in the event that the other party/parties is/are unable to pay.) All the banks have wicked documents called 'joint and several' guarantees. At the time when you sign them there might be an overdraft facility of $100,000 for the company. When further accommodations are granted to the company the debt position grows and grows and the guarantee, because of its wording, picks it all up and passes it back to the guarantors in the way of liability. Generally, the banks want to be able to hold any one person liable for the whole amount.

If you resign your company directorship and/or sell out of a company, you should make sure you obtain a release from any guarantees you have signed. Under favourable circumstances, banks will usually release one director who is leaving the company, provided they get a guarantee from the new director who is coming in and provided he or she is financially viable. If the bank won't release you, at least notify the bank that you are exiting and that you will not be liable for any further credit extended to the company to which you have not given your express consent. That at least gives the bank notice that you are no longer there. A bank generally will give notice about extending further credit to a company in those circumstances, notwithstanding the terms of your guarantee; however, the bank can extend credit to the company on any terms it likes and you are liable whether you know about it or otherwise. You could at least muster an argument against the bank that it ought not to rely on your guarantee to the extent of any further credit extended after the date on which you gave the bank notice that you exited.

The other documents that banks use and that ought to be avoided if at all possible are what are called Deeds of Cross-collateralisation or Deeds of Cross-covenant. Where a small business has a number of operating entities within a group — that is, perhaps two or three companies operating different facets of the business — there may be assets held in several of the entities and not just in one. If one of the companies is the borrowing entity, the banks may use these very powerful documents to bring every company within the net so that each becomes a guarantor of the other.

A lawyer told me recently of a case in which a company that is now in liquidation had a variety of facilities from the bank and certain properties were mortgaged in relation to those facilities. His client, who was a director of the company, tried to argue that a particular property secured a particular facility and no other. This produced adverse financial repercussions because a couple of properties were worth more than the loan facility that they secured and some less. On the face of the documents the court rejected his argument and lumped all properties together to cover all liabilities because the guarantee was worded 'all monies'.

CASE STUDY:

Peter went into business in used cars. Although he was a very good salesman, he wasn't very good at managing his business, as is often the case. He was good at talking to customers but paid no attention to detail. He went about

---

willy nilly, signing personal guarantees without really understanding the ramifications. Peter signed joint and several guarantees, he signed cross-collateral guarantees and cross-covenants for the various car yards that he developed as he went along. He had personal guarantees on the floor plan for his cars. He leased hire purchase equipment. Things were going well when the economy was all right. But when things started to go bad Peter found that he wasn't making enough sales and the sales he was making were at vastly reduced prices so the gross profit was down. He had enough stock to cover his creditors, but he didn't have enough to pay the rent on the building or to cover the equipment that he had hired or the floor plan. Even though he thought he had protected himself and had his assets separated, he soon discovered the catastrophic effect of the documents he had signed. He hadn't read the fine print. He has since sworn black and blue that if anyone puts a pen in his hand he will use it only to scratch his back.

Family property should be completely quarantined from the business. It needn't be owned by a separate legal entity altogether — it is usually in the name of the spouse — as long as whoever owns the property isn't going to be liable in any way to anybody as a result of the operations to the company.

CASE STUDY:

According to a recent press article, Australia's best known bankrupt, Bob Ansett, bitterly resents the fact that he was forced to sign personal guarantees to get financial support from lenders and suppliers for his car rental business. His personal assets are now under scrutiny, despite the fact that they are jointly owned by his wife, who was not a director of his company and did not sign any guarantees. According to the article, his creditors, who believe that their losses might have been less had Ansett recognised and faced up to his problems sooner, have put a caveat on his house so that if it is sold they are entitled to the proceeds from Ansett's half share.

In marriages where property is jointly owned and one partner is, if you like, a shelter and hasn't given guarantees and isn't liable to creditors, the parties may be able to go to the Family Court and get a decision in relation to their respective rights and entitlements in property. They might then be able to have property transferred from one party to another under order by the Court or by registering an agreement which has the same effect. (Obviously it is better planning from the start to have the material assets in the name of the spouse not involved in the business.) The down side to this is that, in the event of separation or divorce, the Family Court will take the ownership of property at face value, regardless of any arrangements for planning purposes or the like. If one partner is the proprietor of the property then that partner retains it in the event of a divorce.

Bankruptcy is fairly wide reaching and you would be foolish to play with scams and schemes to dispose of assets. Ideas such as selling all your assets to a totally independent person may work but they can just as easily be set aside. The law will tighten up in this area as it becomes increasingly used and its weaknesses disclosed.

At all times avoid the legal minefield. If you are caught in this respect, you can only blame yourself. Either you didn't read the fine print, or you didn't pay enough attention to detail, or you didn't plan ahead. Address your problems — whether to do with partnerships, customers, employees, creditors, or whatever — as and when they occur; don't allow them to fester and grow out of proportion. In this respect the Japanese seem to have themselves worked out: they have quite a lot of business schools and hardly any law firms.

Make an effort to resolve disputes before the need for legal action arises: talk the issues through, come to an agreement, even if there is a cost involved. A far greater cost, without doubt, is that of getting embroiled in the legal system. This is quicksand for small businesses, and it is unknown territory — once you get in, you will have little chance of getting out unscathed. The only winner of the game is the legal system itself. The costs to you are time, cash, worry and disruption of the stability of your personal and business life. If you do require the services of a solicitor, for example when planning a business agreement, or, indeed, when trying to settle a dispute, gather all documentation and establish a legal framework yourself before making contact. Instruct the solicitor specifically in your requirements rather than asking for advice. Advice not only attracts a higher fee but it also means that you do not own the decision that it prompts. And finally, remember that you need a legal 'GP' as well as access to a number of specialists, just as you do medically.

CHAPTER 8

On the Brink

Business failure is a fact of life during periods of recession, and its incidence is increasing all the time. Bankruptcies in Australia have risen from about 1300 in 1974–75 to 5000 in 1982–83 and 8500 in 1989–90 (fifteen per cent more than the previous year). The figures for 1990–91 are expected to double, with those for the second quarter already fifty-six per cent higher than for the first. The real tragedy in these statistics is that a high proportion of all bankruptcies could, and should, have been avoided.

Apart from the general problem of bad management, the main specific cause of small business collapse is acknowledged to be the simple failure to keep proper records. As we have seen, business operators need to watch five key indicators in order to know how they are travelling: the level of turnover, the level of debtors at any time, the level of creditors, the value of stock and the level of bank overdraft. By tracking the movement of those five things — and they needn't be reconciled in a double entry system — from one period to the next they can work out whether they are getting into trouble or whether they are going along profitably.

In the absence of proper records, business operators often don't prepare budgets, they don't plan ahead. Or, if they do prepare budgets, they don't compare actual performance with budget to find out how they are going. Too often, if they fall short of sales budget, they might look for the reasons, but if they exceed sales budget they often simply say 'That's good' and don't look at why. But, as we saw in chapter 6, a better-than-budget result is frequently due to factors quite separate from those which were planned; and if you don't analyse both the gains and the deficiencies you really don't know where you are going. The business might have picked up a very significant order from one sector of the economy, giving it better turnover and profitability for a particular quarter, but this might be a once-in-a-blue-moon shot and in fact the business might be going down, with the decline being masked by the windfall.

Perception is also a common problem. Because of their characteristic optimism, too many enterprisers refuse to accept that things are turning down or going badly. They have not worked for a salary or a wage and gone home every day at five o'clock; they eat and sleep their business, and they have probably involved their family as well. They are too close to make an objective assessment of the situation. They don't want to recognise the danger signs because they can't accept that these probably reflect on their own management. A by-product of this is introspection — looking too closely at your business at the expense of knowing what is going on around you.

MAKING THE HARD DECISIONS

Don't let bankruptcy creep up on you. Act to prevent it. Tough times call for hard decisions and these cover the whole spectrum of the business plan, from the decision to get out in the field and spend more time with your customers, to the decision to work more hours, perhaps even spend less time at home. It is hard to retrench staff or reduce their wages, to delay payment to creditors, to dare to go and sit in people's offices and collect your money, to upset people in the short term for the sake of long-term survival. It is hard to get rid of surplus equipment, not to buy equipment that you believe you need, to replace a new car with a second-hand one, to get rid of surplus stock at a price lower than it is worth. Certainly it is hard to cut your own wages and adopt a more moderate lifestyle. It is hard to go to the bank manger and ask for extended credit, to maintain tight cash control. All these are hard decisions; and in tough times they crop up more frequently than usual and their effect is more critical.

Look at ways of minimising waste. This should be second nature in all economic climates, not just when things are tough; and if undertaken as a team effort it can be quite a challenge. Obviously every business is different, and the following list of suggestions is offered as a starting point only. I hope it will stimulate you to come up with your own ideas.

- Investigate Telecom's TIM (Telephone Internal Monitoring) system which provides you with details of all calls made.
- Don't let your staff fill their tanks on Fridays or Mondays with petrol supplied by the company unless they have special approval.
- Pay a car allowance rather than buy a new vehicle.
- Where possible give products as a promotional tool rather than non-deductible gifts or cash.
- Constantly monitor your use of couriers compared with mail, facsimile and phone. Indiscriminate use of couriers is expensive.
- Monitor the cost effectiveness of mobile telephones. Are they really essential for an organised sales professional or representative?
- Continually re-appraise company cars and equipment supplied to staff.
- All samples, gifts or products used internally should be invoiced against the relevant account to enable control and appraisal and avoid abuse.
- If you have a large number of interstate suppliers, consider asking them to obtain 008 telephone numbers. If they are not prepared to do so, suggest that they ring you rather than you ring them.
- Monitor freight alternatives. There are so many

different methods: bus, rail, post, independent trucking, courier and your own transport. Choices change with size, quantity and style of goods. Watch how you categorise your deliveries because some companies charge on mass, where weight would be much more competitive depending on the category of goods. Carefully check every invoice you receive from a freight company as they are renowned for promising one thing at the initial contract stage and delivering another at the invoice stage.

- If you use writing pads turn them glued end towards you and write from the cut edge down, using a ruler to tear off only the piece you have used. The paper will go a lot further.
- Recycle wasted or obsolete photocopies by using the other side. Create a store of scrap paper from old files. Ask your bank manager for free scraps of pads or cut waste paper into pads. It sounds tight, but watching the pennies ensures that the pounds will look after themselves.
- Many used envelopes can be neatly recycled by covering the old address with a stick-on label.
- Never throw out anything with a paperclip or butterfly clip still attached.
- Set a donation schedule at the beginning of the year. This avoids random donations by anyone on your staff or by yourself in a weak moment. Another idea is to offer charities stock at cost price rather than making a monetary donation.
- Check size and effectiveness of computer reports. Large unnecessary reports are not user friendly and they waste paper and equipment time as well as taking longer to read.
- Do you really need packing slips? And can't your invoices serve simultaneously as statements? Sending out statements is an unnecessary cost which actually delays the payment of the invoice. It

is common these days to eliminate the statement process and request payment against invoice. Try to limit any unnecessary processes of this type.

Be tough but don't be impetuous. For example, think twice before slashing your marketing budget, no matter how tempting this might be. Tough times offer fertile ground for the enterprising marketer. While your competitors are pulling their horns in, you can be out there scooping up opportunities that they have let go. A recent report published in the United States showed that, rather than reduce spending on advertising during hard times, businesses can profit by at least maintaining their normal allowance. The sales and net profit performance of 133 companies were compared, some of which reduced advertising expenditure in the 1974–75 recession. The study showed that companies that did not cut advertising fared much better during and after the recession than those that did, because they maintained market share and brand awareness. Using advertising to gain an edge over your competitors may be less expensive in real dollars in uncertain times than it is in good times, when more companies maintain a strong profile. Take advantage of the fact that many sellers of advertising space actually reduce their rates during bad times to attract customers. And if you still need to reduce advertising costs, rather than decide not to advertise at all, you might look at the possibility of doing your own. Any advertising undertaken in this climate must be very accurately targeted.

Also be careful if you are forced by tight cashflow requirements to lay off staff and pay out large lump sums. You should make yourself aware of your legal obligations as an employer and provide some sort of counselling, whether internal or external, to the displaced personnel. (Reflecting the current economic climate, a new consultancy industry has sprung up to assist retrenched staff to re-establish their careers and minimise the negative effects of retrenchment on individuals and organisations. Employers are counselled before the termination interview, and the staff in question are assessed and supported afterwards.) Adequate notice should be given, in writing and at least in line with the frequency of payment (if payment is monthly give one month's warning or if it is weekly give one week's warning). Quite often employers will make a payment in lieu of notice. The advantage of this is that it prevents the disgruntled employee from undermining the owner and causing an upset with clients. The disadvantage is that it could cause industrial problems. Explain that the retrenchment is necessary to protect the jobs of the other staff and to enable the business to survive. Presuming it is the case, point out that you have applied the principle of 'last in, first to go', as a matter of fairness. Where applicable involve the union, for advice and assistance.

And finally, don't sell assets which dramatically affect the immediate and long-term future productivity or profitability of the business. It is also important wherever possible not to sell real estate assets. Concentrate on selling those assets which are superfluous and non-productive and don't enhance your income. Try to hang on to your home asset particularly because it is a tax-free investment and you can always borrow against it as security. Banks prefer bricks and mortar security like that.

ASSESSING THE SITUATION

Once you have considered and made all the available hard decisions, you will be in a position to isolate problems that are specific to your business from those of the wider economic environment. If it is clear at this stage that you are unable comfortably to meet your commitments when they fall due and your business is sliding into trouble, act immediately. The sooner you act, the better the chance that you will be able to trade out of your problems with the support of your creditors and bankers.

Start by calling in a specialist accountant (see pages 105–6). As your own management skills will at this stage, fairly or unfairly, be judged to be lacking, the accountant will be able to provide some sort of external credibility by objectively researching your financial affairs.

Once your accountant has investigated your situation in detail he or she will prepare a report, including a detailed statement of position, and advise you on which way to go next. The accountant will probably start by identifying where losses are occurring, will make recommendations on how to reverse them, will regain control over cashflow and will then implement tighter credit control, particularly if debtors are not paying or are paying slowly, or if there are some potential bad debts. He/she will place controls over stock and production, making sure that stock is being turned over and there is no excess, and will obviously review and try to reduce overheads.

The scope of the accountant's report will vary according to the business, but obviously it will state what the immediate cash requirements are, what the latest asset and liability statement is and what forecasts are available. Its purpose will be to establish whether your business is viable, and if so to what extent, and to decide on a course of action.

The accountant's report will answer the following questions: What is the business predicament at the moment? How serious are the problems? Can the employees be paid? Is there adequate insurance to cover all the assets? Which creditors are essential to the continuation of the business? Are there any legal actions? Is there any action or threat of action to repossess any essential assets? If the premises are rented what is the status of your lease? Do you have any equipment that is subject to a usage-or-return agreement? Are there any forward supply commitments that can be cancelled? Have any other things occurred that are peculiar to the business? Most importantly, what is the tax position? What money is owed to the Commissioner for Taxation? (Keep him happy and paid up, because he is never sympathetic or slow to take legal action.) This all takes time and makes demands on your stressed short-term memory, but your files should supply you with much of the information needed for this crucial document.

Establish your exact cash/bank position. Gather the facts, list the monthly totals of receipts and payments for the last twelve months from the bank statements. If the cash book is up to date and the bank reconciliation completed, verify the above figures. List all unpaid creditors and isolate those who have to be paid to keep the doors open. Sort the rest according to commercial priority and descending dollar value.

Determine any forward order commitments, particularly overseas, and any bills payable. Review the debtors listing. Test the age analysis (30, 60, 90 days, and so on). Are slow-paying debtors significant? Which of these are also good customers? Examine the correspondence file for incidents of complaints. They could signal a bad debt. Send out some random debtor statements for verification. Complete a physical stocktake. Get opinions from storemen as to the slowness of stock or out-of-balance items. Note any items that could be disposed of. Obtain valuations for fixed and other assets. List all hire purchase, leasing, property rentals and advertising commitments. Schedule the payments, particularly any periodical payments. Check the last group tax paid. This is a notorious deferred liability. Verify your standings from payrolls. List employee holiday pay, long service leave and any deferred commission. Determine the unpaid income tax position.

Your accountant will ask you for all the details as to which assets are owned by whom and in whose name. Is there anything held in trust for third parties? Has anything been disposed of within the last two years (or two to five years if you have been insolvent before)? The Bankruptcy Act is very strong and has the ability to call back any voluntary dispositions or disposals at less than full value for the benefit of the creditors or lenders or whoever is entitled to be paid. The Act (new Section 139(a)) basically allows the court to determine any asset which is not necessarily owned in the name of the bankrupt, but which is held by third parties and which can be said to be in control of the bankrupt to be repossessed and used to pay out creditors.

Once you have established and documented your financial position in this way, some important questions must be asked by way of deciding whether or not you can survive:

1 What is the actual reason for the company's decline?
2 What is the severity of the crisis?
3 What is the attitude of the shareholders/bankers/creditors?

4 What are the industry's characteristics — its products, its market, its competitors?
5 What has been the company's traditional marketing strategy?
6 What is the company's cost price structure and its gross profit margin?
7 What external events may assist or detract from recovery?

If the situation appears beyond redemption, the accountant will recommend that you consider winding up; if recovery seems possible, the accountant will recommend that you trade out of your current difficulties. The former solution is dealt with in part 4. The latter will depend on the support of your creditors and lenders.

SURVIVING

Your first step on the road to recovery is to use all the information from your statement of position to re-do the budget and cashflow forecasts. Then ascertain who can be paid and how much. What do you have to collect and when? Develop a check list. Has the business got any cash in it? What is the overdraft limit? Are there any unpaid cheques? Are there any cheques or cash to be banked? Is there any available cash just for banking?

The next thing to do is to find out what the business has to pay out over the next month. Estimate wages. Add up creditors due. Assess your own drawings and resolve not to take so much out. Find out whether any other payments are to be made. Next, calculate how much money is to come in from cash sales, from payment by debtors or any other income. Then decide how much money is needed to survive.

Good management is critical to the successful planning and implementation of a turnaround, particularly if you are to keep your staff and motivate them during this uncertain period. Bear in mind that the rescue will generally take longer than anticipated and initial assessments will frequently underestimate the degree of change required.

The turnaround might be possible using your existing management structure, whether it be yourself or others, or it might require the appointment of a new chief executive or at least a new external, specialised accountant. The latter would certainly indicate your serious intentions and give some credibility to your rescue attempt. It may also give some confidence to the creditors and leave you to pay them back in good time. There is a general belief that the owner of a business who trades it into serious financial crisis is probably not the one who will be able to trade it out of it. Obviously the choice of chief executive/ accountant is most important. You would look for people in your industry who have been successful before. If that person was available, less time would be taken to settle in. Given the need to operate at a fast pace in the turnaround environment where there is tremendous pressure to achieve results in the shortest possible time, a good manager from elsewhere in the industry may be less attractive than an outsider with successful turn-around experience, for example the same person who prepared your initial investigation and statement of position.

Businesses which have experienced financial difficulties and have weak financial cashflow control systems will initially depend on gaining control over cash, preparing short-term forecasts, preparing detailed operating budgets and reviewing all manufacturing and overhead expenditures. Effective systems in these areas need to be operational within weeks to establish control and direction.

Generally businesses in severe financial crisis will need to look at recovery as a process consisting of two stages whose order cannot be reversed. The first stage generally entails contracting and rationalising your business back to a profitable cell. The second is to move towards growth-orientated strategies to build a sustained recovery.

In a financial crisis the ideal action is often surgical in nature. The operation may withdraw from whole business areas — by closure, divesting or sale, and by limitation of product lines and/or customers which on careful analysis are unprofitable or where return on investment is poor. This cuts the operation back to its core so it can be profitable again.

Once your core business is re-established, issues such as the pricing policy can be looked at again. Perhaps you can increase prices. It therefore becomes critical to understand the competitive situation and price elasticity or demand for major product categories. As I have already said, most small businesses underprice themselves. They are surprised to discover that even when they increase their prices, sometimes dramatically, they don't lose customers but in fact gain them. Elasticity means that, theoretically, if the price of your product goes up demand will go down. Whereas, an inelastic product is one where the price goes up but the product demand also goes up.

More attention should be paid to providing your existing customers with a total and proper service, ideally resulting in an improved selling effort, and to concentrating on those customers who will generate most of the profit.

A company in financial crisis will also seek to return to profitability through reduction of costs, but it also needs to generate cash. Therefore one of the strategies in the early days of the survival plan is to identify which assets are surplus and which assets are going to be necessary for the future profitability of the business. Sell the surplus to gain some cash.

Tactics used in an asset reduction strategy could include elimination of product lines which are unprofitable and/or unnecessary, sale of subsidiaries or branches that do not meet profitable requirements or fit the company's refocussed product market objectives, sale of under-utilised or surplus fixed assets, sale and lease-back of land, buildings and/or plant, reducing working capital requirements by improving inventory (that is, stock), reducing your stock and collecting your money more quickly and having fewer debtors. Obviously, cutting back costs is most important. This could be done through repurchasing, buying more cheaply or finding alternative sources to buy from. It could also come from better utilisation of materials and by substituting materials.

Keep your staff on side during these difficult times — reassure them, be honest with them, talk openly with them — because you will need them to trade out of your difficulties. It is critical to run mean and lean in the crucial stage of the recovery plan.

Unilateral thinking is required. Once all the costs have been cut back to a minimum and you have got your core business profitable again it may be a wise idea to protect yourself in the future by growing by acquisition of another company. One needs to be very careful in this area, though.

Alternatively, the accountant's report may have revealed the need for an initial injection of funds, therefore new shareholders may be found or joint venture partners may be sought to provide necessary capital to bring the business back to profitability. If this is not desirable, you might consider the possibility of finding an 'angel', or someone who will buy your business from you at a reasonable price rather than becoming a partner. This again revolves around preparing a business plan and making sure the presentation is honest.

Normally, businesses in financial crisis are overborrowed. This can have a crippling effect, particularly when interest rates are high. Debt restructuring and other financial strategies can form part of the overall rescue package, for example, the use of asset reduction strategies can assist in the reduction of borrowing levels. The success of any debt restructuring would depend on the new management's ability to convince financiers and other interested parties and creditors that the appropriate rescue plan has been actioned and the prospect of recovery is sound.

Some other ideas are to:

- change your financiers (often if a company has gone through a difficult period it tends to lose credibility with existing lenders. Coupled with the new top management/accountant and the development of a recovery unit it may be advantageous to consider an alternative financier);
- consolidate funding (the company in a crisis will often have a proliferation of funding agreements with a number of different financiers, leases and hire purchases all over the place. In order to reduce the overall cost you might be wiser to convert short-term debt to longer term facilities, to include current outstanding interest in the new loan facility

and to arrange for sale and lease-back of property and equipment);
- raise additional loans or convert existing loans to equity;
- raise additional capital;
- if possible, obtain financial assistance from government (highly unlikely in tough times).

Above all, as I have said so many times in this book, it is important to keep everyone informed, particularly your bank and creditors, and be honest. Of course, this should be happening anyway. But, it is particularly important when you are reading the danger signs and discover that your business is in trouble. Understand that your bank and your creditors don't want to sell you up; they want to continue their business with you because you are their customer. If you get into trouble you will jeopardise not only the money you owe them but also future profits in terms of interest or future trading with your creditors.

To sum up, the action plan for a business staging a recovery is:
- Divest yourself of surplus stock. Convert it into cash, or bail your way out of assets that have limited economic use. This includes personal assets. Perhaps the caravan that you haven't used for years can be traded in for a utility truck or a facsimile machine which would be useful in your business.
- Analyse what stock sells and in what quantities. Too much stock costs money. Too little stock loses money. Stock control is critical.
- Look at restructuring your loan portfolio and your lines of credit before the crunch really hits you. Ensure that you have adequate cash to draw on. Investigate how you are using your assets as security. Banks and financiers love nothing better than to have a small advance against a property with substantial worth. Most properties, including your house, can be geared to about eighty per cent of

valuation. Attempt to get larger unsecured lines of credit, such as larger Bankcard, Visa or Mastercard lines. Consider discretionary, unsecured, flexible overdraft facilities — rainy-day money which you may never need but which is in place when you require it. The worst time to look for money is when your back is to the wall.

- Reduce staff numbers. Let go those who do not contribute directly to the money-making function of the business. Retain your good-quality people. You might have to be ruthless — if not, you could jeopardise the jobs of *all* your employees.

- Review all your overhead expenditures. Get rid of those that are not producing an economic return. Subscriptions to the local health club are fine in good times, but are questionable in the belt-tightening period. Look at tightening the screws on capital expenditure. Re-assess your spending priorities.

- Collect from your debtors. Review office procedures for the collection of cash, particularly debtors. In the ordering of goods and services examine the credit worthiness of your customers. Review the cost of producing goods and services that you sell. Look for cost savings, look for assistance from your suppliers — they might agree to a slightly longer payment period. Let's face it, they have a vested interest in your survival. Above all look for the right price for the right goods and service from suppliers who are likely to weather the storm themselves.

- Get back to the basics of the business. Stick to what you know best. Identify your core products or services, identify your market strengths, examine your competitors and their efforts to cope with tougher times. Conserve cash wherever and whenever you can. If necessary, extend existing leasing terms to defer large pay-outs of unproductive cash, such as long-service leave.

- Look after and service your customers.

PART FOUR: GETTING OUT

CHAPTER 9

Insolvency

If the investigator's report has shown your ailing business to be insolvent and all bids to save it have failed, you must consider your final options, some of which will enable you to stay in business.

AVAILABLE OPTIONS

There are various types of insolvency administrations. You will need to consult a specialist lawyer and/or accountant about which one is appropriate to your circumstances.

For company structures the options are: a Scheme of Arrangement, receivership and liquidation.

A **Scheme of Arrangement** is an arrangement whereby the company's creditors agree to a moratorium on their debts to enable the company to continue to trade. A Scheme of Arrangement should never be undertaken without specialist advice and assistance. In some cases, to give creditors confidence to accept an arrangement, a scheme manager may be appointed to oversee the operations of the company and report on its performance. A formal Scheme of Arrangement is one approved by the creditors and the court. Obtaining the necessary approval can be expensive and time-consuming. An informal Scheme of Arrangement can be made, provided *all* creditors agree. This operates as a contract between all the creditors and the company. Unless all creditors are parties to the contract, an uncooperative creditor who is not a party could proceed to wind up the company and this would, of course, bring the scheme undone.

In **receivership** a receiver or receiver-manager is usually appointed by a secured creditor pursuant to a Debenture Charge over some or all of the company's assets. The Debenture Charge may or may not give the receiver-manager the power to carry on the business of the company. Sometimes a Debenture Charge is simply a fixed charge on one particular asset of the company, such as an item of equipment or a vehicle. In such a case the receiver's powers are limited to that asset and would normally involve his selling the asset.

Whenever a secured creditor proposes to appoint a receiver or a receiver-manager an important consideration is whether there is any group tax owing to the Federal Commissioner of Taxation. If there is, this must be paid first out of the assets in the hands of the receiver or receiver-manager. Certain alternative (sometimes called 'creative') appointments have been developed whereby, for example, the appointed receiver is not in possession of all the company's assets and the group tax liability can be avoided. If a secured creditor appoints an agent to take possession of and deal with the company's assets, the appointee is known as the agent for the mortgagee in possession.

If you have acted early in recognising trouble and appointing a receiver-manager to take over from your investigating accountant, your business might gain much-needed breathing space to trade out of its difficulties. In this sense the receiver-manager is more like a doctor tending a sick patient than an undertaker preparing a body for burial. The time can be used to investigate the company's operations and to develop a business plan which takes it back to being a going concern. This may involve selling off unprofitable parts of the business or introducing equity. If you apply to the court for the appointment of a receiver yourself, you might have a better chance of obtaining a moratorium on payments to creditors.

When a receiver-manager is appointed he will carry out his

own investigation to ascertain the company's real position, and this can take from two days to six weeks. He will then place appropriate controls over all the key aspects of the business, including ordering systems, accounting systems, payment systems, cash receipts and banking and stock. If the business is to continue as a going concern the receiver will develop budgets with a view to survival. A receiver will be reluctant to trade on in a company unless the outcome is reasonably certain. This is because the receiver renders himself personally liable for goods and services acquired and other contracts entered into by him during the course of the receivership. He needs to ensure that he can satisfy those obligations out of the company's cashflow.

Being in receivership is a new and worrying experience for many company directors, and also for customers and suppliers, particularly if the business depends on continuous supply. The receiver will endeavour to re-establish confidence in the company's customers and suppliers and to reassure them of eventual payment for any goods and services provided during the course of the receivership. The directors of a company in receivership have only limited powers and must observe certain statutory obligations. Responsibility for the day-to-day running of the business lies with the receiver, who may choose to dispense with the services of the directors.

It is important to remember that the appointment of a receiver or a receiver-manager by a secured creditor does not prevent the company's being placed in liquidation if it is insolvent. In the event of liquidation, the liquidator would not have recourse to any of the assets charged in favour of the secured creditor by the Debenture Charge. The liquidator is the representative of the unsecured creditors. He would, for example, have the power to investigate the conduct of the receiver in the administration of the company's assets as well as the validity of the receiver's appointment.

Liquidation is the last step which precedes the dissolution of a company. A liquidator appointed to a company is charged with the orderly realisation of its assets and the distribution of the proceeds to creditors and, if there is any surplus, to shareholders. The liquidator's powers include carrying on the business of the company, but only insofar as that is necessary to ultimately wind up the company.

There are several types of liquidation. *Members' voluntary liquidation* usually occurs when the company's members consider it redundant but it is able to pay all its liabilities in full. *Creditors' voluntary liquidation* usually occurs when the company is unable to pay its debts in full and the members decide to liquidate. *Court liquidation* is usually commenced by a creditor as a result of an unsatisfied demand for a debt which is then due and payable. The demand must be for a debt in excess of one thousand dollars and, if the company is unable to pay or otherwise satisfy the debt within a period of three weeks after the demand is made, the creditor can apply to the court for a winding up order against the company. Where the directors of a company realise that the company is hopelessly insolvent and should be wound up immediately, the members of the company can resolve to apply to the court for the winding up of the company forthwith. It is customary for the company to seek the appointment of a *provisional liquidator* until the winding up order is made by the court and a formal liquidator is appointed. The appointment of a provisional liquidator may also be sought by a creditor, particularly where the court is satisfied that such an appointment is necessary to control and protect the assets of the company and thus the interests of all creditors. If there is evidence that the company was insolvent at the time of the application and has been dissipating its assets, then the court is likely to grant the appropriate order.

The liquidator's function is to collect and realise the assets of the company and distribute the proceeds in the order required by law. The liquidator may deal only with the unsecured assets of the company, first paying any unremitted tax to the Commissioner of Taxation. Protection is also offered to employees in respect of unpaid wages, holiday pay and long-service leave entitlements. Many awards also include redundancy payments. The liquidator has wide powers of investigation of the company's activities and the conduct of its officers.

In the case of voluntary liquidations, the liquidator must be properly qualified (generally as an accountant who is a member of the Institute of Chartered Accountants in Australia or the Australian Society of Accountants) and registered. In the case of court liquidations, the liquidator must be an official liquidator who is registered as such. All official liquidators are listed on a court roster system and are the only liquidators entitled to be appointed by the court. Liquidators' fees are based on hourly rates as set down by the Insolvency Practitioners' Association. Any fees charged by the liquidator out of the assets of a company are usually subject to scrutiny by the court.

For sole proprietors and partnerships (or guarantors who are caught and simply cannot meet their legal, if not moral, obligations), the main insolvency administrations are governed by the Bankruptcy Act 1966 (as amended) and fall into two categories:
- formal bankruptcy, either entered into voluntarily by the debtor at his/her own instigation or involuntarily at the suit of a creditor or creditors;
- arrangements outside of formal bankruptcy, often referred to as Part X (i.e. ten) arrangements — i.e. a Deed of Compromise, a Deed of Assignment or a Deed of Arrangement.

Under a **formal bankruptcy** (voluntary or involuntary) all your divisible property becomes the property of the official trustee who, in the case of hopelessly bankrupt persons, is a government appointee and, in other cases, is a registered trustee and usually an independent accountant. Under formal bankruptcy the debtor does not lose all his/her property. He/she is entitled to retain sufficient personal income, family allowances and pensions as are necessary for support; beds, fittings, personal items of clothing, tools of trade up to the value of $500, property held in trust for another person and the benefits of insurance policies and damages receivable for personal injuries. The role of the trustee is to gather in the divisible property of the debtor to realise that property and to divide the proceeds amongst the creditors according to priority set down by the law.

Whilst you are a bankrupt you are not allowed to be a director or public officer of a company or act in any senior management role in a company. This places severe restrictions on you. Your financial affairs remain in the hands of the official trustee and you may be required to notify him periodically of any income you receive. Any surplus over and above that needed to support yourself (and family, if applicable) may have to be paid to the trustee to be applied in favour of your creditors. If you are employed, your employer may be ordered to pay over any part of your income that exceeds your normal support requirements.

As a bankrupt you are prohibited from obtaining credit above a nominal amount without first disclosing that you are a bankrupt. If you open a bank account, you must report this to the trustee. Infringement of many of the restrictions imposed upon you as a bankrupt is punishable, possibly incurring a prison sentence. Offences committed during bankruptcy may delay your ultimate discharge from it. Normally, unless offences have occurred or your trustee or any creditor objects, you will be automatically discharged from bankruptcy after three years. On discharge, you are released from all provable debts which were in existence when you were made a bankrupt.

It is important to remember that if your spouse is not made a bankrupt he or she is treated as a separate individual and his or her property is not available in your bankruptcy for the benefit of creditors. For example, if you jointly own your home, only your share passes to the official trustee. Without the co-operation of your spouse the trustee will have some difficulty in dealing with your interest in the property. Usually, however, a spouse will co-operate with the trustee in selling the property, repaying any mortgage debt and sharing in the proceeds on an equal basis. The non-bankrupt spouse would be entitled to retain his or her share of the proceeds from the sale. Your spouse is not prevented from running the business while you are a bankrupt and he or she may employ you to assist in the operation of the business. However, great care must be exercised to ensure that the business is owned by the spouse, otherwise the business may also become an asset available to the bankrupt's creditors.

If you are a bankrupt, your creditors are entitled to conduct an examination of your assets and affairs on oath before the Registrar in Bankruptcy. These examinations are generally undertaken where creditors are suspicious that not all the assets of the bankrupt have been disclosed to the trustee or that there may have been transactions which, with further detail, the trustee may have set aside to recover monies or property disposed of by the bankrupt prior to bankruptcy.

If you have dealt fairly and frankly with your creditors you have a greater chance of avoiding formal bankruptcy and winning the creditors' support for an arrangement outside bankruptcy. Proposals for such arrangements are notified to your creditors who are invited to attend a meeting at which you will be present, together with a person, known as a controlling trustee (or a solicitor), whom you have authorised to convene the meeting of your creditors. The granting of the authority to the controlling trustee is of itself an act of bankruptcy which would entitle a creditor or creditors who are owed more than $1500 to bring a petition for your bankruptcy. At the meeting of creditors your proposals are placed before the creditors, who vote on whether the proposal should be accepted or rejected. If rejected the meeting may require you to file a bankruptcy petition within seven days.

Of the three **arrangements outside bankruptcy,** the *Deed of Compromise* is the simplest, whereby creditors agree to accept either a once-and-for-all payment of a lesser sum in full satisfaction of all liabilities, or a periodic payment. Creditors are unlikely to accept less than the full amount of their debt unless they are satisfied that there are no available assets or income which would give them a better return. They need to be convinced that they would not fare better under a formal bankruptcy. How you win their support will vary according to your personal circumstances. Sometimes a monetary contribution by a third party, such as a member of your family, over and above what you are able to provide for yourself may be sufficient to convince the creditors that you have done your best.

The *Deed of Assignment* is very similar to formal bankruptcy, in that under the Deed you assign and transfer to a trustee for distribution to the creditors all your existing assets which would be available if you were made formally bankrupt. The main advantage of this arrangement over formal bankruptcy is that you may still remain a director of a company and act in the management of the company. Under a Deed of Compromise or a Deed of Arrangement you are not able to act as a director or take part directly or indirectly in the management of a company unless the court permits.

The *Deed of Arrangement* is any arrangement which the creditors agree upon which is neither a Deed of Assignment nor a Deed of Compromise. It may involve a combination of the two and other arrangements as well. The Deed of Arrangement normally envisages a continuity of business with either interim or ultimate returns to the creditors either in part or in full.

For any of the arrangements outside bankruptcy to be accepted, you need to obtain a vote of the creditors in support of the arrangement of at least seventy-five per cent in value — that is, what is owed to those creditors — and at least fifty per cent of the number of creditors.

The law in relation to bankruptcy and Part X arrangements is very complex. Before contemplating any insolvency administration you should ensure that you obtain specialist advice. The main advantages of an arrangement outside bankruptcy are:

- It doesn't carry the stigma of bankruptcy.
- Except in the case of a Deed of Assignment you are not subject to public examination before the Registrar in Bankruptcy.
- Your creditors do not generally have access to any property which you acquired after entering into the arrangement.
- Your future income is usually protected.
- There are fewer potential criminal liabilities than in the case of formal bankruptcy.
- Provided you can win the support of the creditors, an arrangement may be made which is more suitable to your personal circumstances.

There are also distinct advantages for your creditors. These are:

- They are likely to fare better under the arrangement than in a formal bankruptcy, particularly if the arrangement envisages a continuity of your business.
- Generally the cost of the administration of the arrangement is less than in the case of formal bankruptcy.

Your credibility will be important. You should consider factors that might improve your bargaining power and persuade creditors to accept your proposal. The controlling trustee selected by you is obliged to advise the creditors whether the trustee considers the proposal is of benefit to the creditors or otherwise. If you deal fully and frankly with your trustee and with your creditors you will increase the chances of an acceptable proposal being made. In this context any attempts to make private arrangements with some creditors and not others can spell disaster. If you pay one creditor and not others you will only antagonise the unpaid creditors. Moreover, any arrangements you do make with individual creditors outside of the provisions of Part X of the Bankruptcy Act are not binding on them and they may still proceed against you.

As in the case of companies, if a creditor is proceeding against you for formal bankruptcy the court has the power to appoint a trustee to preserve your assets and business until the petition is heard by the court. If, for example, you were dissipating assets, paying creditors or removing monies from the business a creditor could seek the appointment of an interim receiver to preserve intact the assets and the business.

CASE STUDY:

A fellow I know purchased a leasehold on a hotel during boom times, more for his ego than for financial benefit. However, he didn't attend to the bottom line as he was more interested in increasing turnover for turnover's

---

sake. When things became difficult he needed to borrow money and went to the bank to increase his overdraft. He provided an up-to-date and accurate statement of his assets and liabilities. Unfortunately the inevitable occurred and, with losses on several negatively geared properties, he found himself unable to meet his commitments. He sought advice too late and filed a Part X, but naively omitted one of the properties which had been included in his previous financial statement, believing this anomaly would not be noticed by his creditors. When the Part X came to its notice, the bank had no hesitation in declaring him formally bankrupt.

LEGAL OBLIGATIONS

As we have seen, certain precautions should have been taken in the planning stages of your business to protect you in the event of financial disaster. Once your business has collapsed, there is very little you can do to alter the course of events, other than superficially minimising your exposure to ruin by being aware of your legal obligations.

Company law imposes clear legal responsibilities on directors and the courts are only too willing to enforce these. Even if you have not provided personal security or a guarantee for your company's liabilities you could nevertheless find yourself personally liable for debts incurred by the company at a time when the company was technically insolvent and you as a director had reasonable cause to believe that the company was unable to pay all its debts as and when they became due. It is often the case that husband and wife are directors, with the husband the active director of the company and the wife playing the role of housekeeper and mother and having little or no involvement in the management and operations of the company. Recent court decisions have reinforced the provisions under company law which impose upon directors certain duties and responsibilities. Directors are obliged to satisfy themselves that certain things in relation to a company are or are not happening. It is not sufficient for a director to stand idly by and allow the company to be managed by others without taking an active role him- or herself.

Acting as a director of a company should not be done lightly. Company law imposes duties upon directors to act in good faith, to act honestly and not to use their position or information to which they are privy by virtue of being a director for their personal benefit or for the benefit of any other person. If, for example, in order to avoid the consequences of insolvency, you set up a second company and attempted to move assets from the insolvent company to the new entity you run a very real risk of being prosecuted under company law. If you are in any doubt about your obligations as a director or about the financial condition of your company you should obtain appropriate specialist legal and accounting advice at the earliest opportunity.

In desperate times otherwise honourable people might be pushed by the sheer stress and anxiety of it all to consider immoral, unethical or downright illegal escapes. Guard against this temptation and make sure you emerge with your integrity intact; it may well be all you have left. You have the rest of your life to contend with and a reputation to protect. Allowing yourself to slip into moral decline, or even criminal behaviour, is therefore short-sighted.

CHAPTER **10**
Starting Again

T here is no doubt that Australian business is in trouble at the moment. Things will be very difficult for at least a year in all sectors, some — for example, the building industry and related industries — more than others. Almost everyone is affected. But we are still not so badly off as people were during the Great Depression. Business people who survived that time know what it is like to shut down their hatches, run on very minimal overheads and continue operating; or what it is like to face up to the inevitability of having to bow out. They know more than anyone else that hard times require personal sacrifice. Follow their example: *never look back, except to learn.*

A friend of mine once said that it is when you are in the midst of a business failure that you should write down the lessons you have learned, and that you should keep this permanent record to read weekly for the rest of your life, to understand fully and to reapply. Most of this book deals with the basic tenets of going into business, being there and staying there. The final part deals with getting out and this brief chapter broaches the optimistic subject of starting again. However, despite all that is written here, I must admit that nothing will be as real and convincing as your own list of lessons learned from direct involvement. Only that list will be stained with the blood, sweat and tears that make every business endeavour a rich and —

even in the wake of failure — rewarding one. The best intentions and all the research in the world can never prepare you for all contingencies. Having faced them once, however, you are certainly forewarned.

CASE STUDY:

Martin, by his own admission, was very creative. He didn't have an eye for detail, so although he could pull projects and people together he could not follow them through. Martin seemed to get bored easily. During the early part of his career he was in printing. Everything he touched turned to gold. He had no trouble finding clients. The equipment, though heavily financed, was being paid for comfortably and he was able to afford a fairly ambitious lifestyle. Things continued to grow. He put on more staff before he needed them, and soon he was employing something like fifty people. He didn't pay much attention to budgets. He didn't like meetings. His accountants and financial controllers were not able to keep a rein on him. He was looking at the overseas market.

Then came the economic decline. Martin found himself with high borrowings, high interest payments on leases and hire purchase, customers who were in trouble and couldn't pay him. He had excessive overheads and he had committed himself to extensive leased premises and signed a number of personal guarantees. Things looked fairly grim.

Then Martin decided to sit down and learn some lessons. He didn't feel sorry for himself like so many people do when they get themselves into financial trouble. He didn't go around blaming other people. He identified a number of weaknesses in the way he had conducted his business. He had not paid enough attention to detail. He had not spent enough time with his employees. He then set about reducing his overheads, maintaining collectible cashflow from selling printing at a profit, reducing his

---

lifestyle dramatically, cutting his own allowances, not spending money unless absolutely necessary, identifying those customers who would pay on time and getting cash payments where possible. He dramatically reduced the size of his business. The only thing that was hurt was his ego, but he never felt sorry for himself. He only looked back to learn.

A business collapse is a cathartic experience for the person responsible. While the pain and the hardship are still fresh you have a perfect opportunity to refocus your priorities in life, to re-evaluate the fundamentals. This time offers you a forced reassessment of whether you should be in business for yourself or whether you are better off being employed by someone else. It is like being given nought out of ten: sure, you have failed; but what matters is what you are going to do about it. There is no virtue in self-pity; you will only lose the respect of all those around you — not only your loved ones but also your business contacts. Above all, try to maintain your pride and integrity, to be honest with everybody. As the saying goes, 'Tough times come and go, but tough people last.' The circumstances which have brought you to this point will pass; but the rest of your life is still ahead of you. If it is known that you have been honest throughout and that you have done the best you possibly could under the circumstances, you will not be judged harshly and plenty of people will still want to deal with you.

Don't waste the experience; use it to start all over again. Begin by reading this book once more. Develop another business plan, do your market research again. Through all this you might have developed some new skills, or even a new product. Many a successful enterpriser has emerged from the ashes of a failed business. There is no shame in adding yourself to the list.

Despite the toughness of the current economic environment, there are enormous opportunities to start from scratch, take over, merge or develop businesses. Scan the 'For Sale' columns, talk to your accountant, read the newspapers, keep your eyes and your imagination open. Now is the time for getting started, not for giving up. The collapse of one business is not the end of the world; it is the perfect recipe for the beginning of another and the chance to make this one more prosperous than the last.

Where to Go for Help

Government Ombudsmen

Commonwealth	(03) 614 3911
Victoria	(03) 670 7151
New South Wales	(02) 206 1000
Queensland	(07) 229 5116
Western Australia	(09) 225 5000
South Australia	(08) 212 5721
ACT	(062) 76 0111
Tasmania	(002) 34 9200
Northern Territory	(089) 81 2626

Australian Securities Commission

(combining former State and Territory Corporate Affairs Commission with Australian Companies and Securities Commission)

Business Centres (company registration and information services):

Melbourne	(03) 280 3500
Geelong	(052) 29 2966
Sydney	(02) 390 3500
Newcastle	(049) 29 4555

Townsville	(077) 21 3885
Brisbane	(07) 360 7900
Gold Coast	(075) 92 2155
Adelaide	(08) 202 8500
Canberra	(062) 47 5011
Hobart	(002) 35 6850
Darwin	(089) 43 0950

Regional Offices (corporate regulation):

Victoria	(03) 280 3200
New South Wales	(02) 390 3200
Queensland	(07) 360 7700
South Australia	(08) 202 8400
ACT	(062) 47 5011
Tasmania	(002) 35 6800
Northern Territory	(089) 43 0900

Australian Institute of Chartered Accountants

Victoria	(03) 602 5844
New South Wales	(02) 290 1344
Queensland	(07) 221 5644
Western Australia	(09) 322 7999
South Australia	(08) 231 5926
ACT	(062) 73 1213
Tasmania	(002) 23 4799

Australian Society of CPAs (Certified Practising Accountants)

Victoria	(03) 606 9606
New South Wales	(02) 262 6200
Queensland	(07) 832 1194
Western Australia	(09) 481 5944
South Australia	(08) 232 3188
ACT	(062) 57 1858
Tasmania	(002) 34 8244

Law Institutes

Victoria	(03) 607 9311
New South Wales	(02) 220 0333
Queensland	(07) 23 3588
Western Australia	(09) 481 0548
South Australia	(08) 51 9972
ACT	(062) 475 7000
Tasmania	(002) 34 4133
Northern Territory	(089) 81 7104

Department of Consumer Affairs

Victoria	(03) 602 8123
New South Wales	(02) 266 8911
Queensland	(07) 227 4909
Western Australia	(09) 222 0666
South Australia	(08) 228 3211
ACT	(062) 75 8378
Tasmania	(002) 30 2662
Northern Territory	(089) 89 5184

Department of Industry, Technology and Resources

Victoria	(03) 412 8000
Queensland	(07) 224 2180
ACT	(062) 77 7580
Tasmania	(002) 20 4095
Northern Territory	(089) 89 6277

Department of Industry, Technology and Commerce

New South Wales	(02) 256 0922

Ministry of Resources

Western Australia   (09) 222 9577

Ministry of Industry, Trade & Technology

South Australia   (08) 210 8333

Other Government or Semi-Government Bodies

Bureau of Industry Economics (publishers of the annual *Small Business Report*)
Department of Trade and Resources:
— Trade Commissioner Service
— Export Development Grants Board
— Export Finance and Insurance Corporation
Commonwealth Scientific and Industrial Research Organisation (CSIRO)
Commonwealth Employment Service (CES)
Australian Information Service
Australian Industrial Research and Development Incentives Board
Australian Industry Development Corporation
Australian Patent Information Service
Australian Taxation Office
Environmental Impact Statement Enquiries Office
Department of Finance
Department of Primary Industry
Office of the Commissioner for Employees' Compensation
Trade Practices Commission
Department of Consumer Affairs
Treasury Department
Weights and Measures Office
Industries Assistance Commission
Prices Justification Tribunal
Temporary Assistance Authority
Australian Conciliation and Arbitration Commission
Export Finance and Insurance Corporation

Trade Associations

Retail Traders' Association
Metal Trades Industry Association
Meat and Allied Trades Federation
Master Builders' Association
Master Grocers' Association
Manufacturers' Agents Association
Pharmacy Guild of Australia
Real Estate Agents' Association
Timber Merchants' Association
Wholesale Spirit Merchants' Association
Housing Industry Association
Australian Chamber of Manufactures
Electrical Contractors' Federation
Hairdressing and Beauty Association
Master Painters' Association

Training

(see local telephone directories)

TAFE Colleges
Sydney: The College of External Studies
Goulburn: Riverina College of Advanced Education
Lismore: Northern Rivers College of Advanced Education
South Australia: O'Halloran Hill College of TAFE
   (3 campuses)
Hobart: Hobart Technical College
Melbourne: Council of Adult Education
   Chadstone: Holmesglen College of TAFE
   Box Hill: Box Hill College of TAFE
   Footscray: Footscray College of TAFE and Footscray
   Institute of Technology
   Hawthorn: Swinburne Institute of Technology
   Moorabbin: Moorabbin College of TAFE
   Preston: Preston College of TAFE
Ballarat: Ballarat School of Mines and Industries Ltd

Bendigo: Bendigo College of TAFE and Bendigo CAE
Frankston: Frankston College of TAFE
Geelong: Gordon College of TAFE
Horsham: Horsham Learning Centre
Mildura: Sunraysia College of TAFE
Sale: Sale Regional Continuing Education Centre
Shepparton: Shepparton College of TAFE
Wangaratta: Wangaratta College of TAFE and Warrnambool
   Institute of Advanced Education
Yallourn: Yallourn College of TAFE
Perth: Education Department of Western Australia

Universities
Melbourne: Melbourne University and Monash University
Geelong: Deakin University
Nathan: Griffith University
La Trobe Valley: Gippsland Institute of Advanced Education
Armidale: University of New England
Brisbane: Queensland University
Adelaide: South Australian College of Advanced Education
Perth: Western Australian Institute of Technology
Rockhampton: Capricornia Institute of Advanced Education
Darwin: Darwin Community Centre
Lismore: Northern Rivers College of Advanced Education
Wagga Wagga: Riverina College of Advanced Education
Warrnambool: Warrnambool Institute of Advanced Education
Launceston: Tasmanian College of Advanced Education
Perth: Murdoch University
Bathurst: Mitchell College of Advanced Education
Toowoomba: Darling Downs Institute of Advanced Education

Small Business Advisory Services

New South Wales:
Office of Small Business
    139 Macquarie Street
    Sydney NSW 2000
    (02) 27 6261

Victoria:
Small Business Development Corporation
    100 Exhibition Street
    Melbourne VIC 3000
    (03) 654 3166
Queensland:
Small Business Corporation
    STC House
    545 Queen Street
    Brisbane QLD 4000
    (07) 834 6789
South Australia:
Small Business Corporation of South Australia
    74 South Terrace
    Adelaide SA 5000
    (08) 212 5344
Western Australia:
Small Business Development Corporation
    553 Hay Street
    Perth WA 6000
    (09) 325 3388
Tasmania:
Small Business Service, Tasmanian Development Authority
    134 Macquarie Street
    Hobart TAS 7000
    (002) 20 6777
Northern Territory:
Small Business Service
    24 Cavanagh Street
    Darwin NT 0800
    (089) 410 811
ACT:
Small Business Bureau
    1st Floor
    Canberra Savings Centre
    Canberra City ACT 2608
    (062) 57 1155

Australian Bureau of Statistics

Victoria	(03) 615 7000
New South Wales	(02) 268 4111
Queensland	(07) 222 6022
Western Australia	(09) 323 5323
South Australia	(08) 237 7555
ACT	(06) 252 7911
Tasmania	(089) 81 5222
Northern Territory	(002) 205 0111

Franchise Advisory Councils

Franchise Management Aust. Pty Ltd	(03) 663 6499
Franchise Development (Melbourne)	(03) 267 7666
Franchise Development (Adelaide)	(08) 364 1898
Howarth Franchising Services	(02) 266 0655
Franchise Counselling Services	(02) 971 2977

Franchise sections within banks:
  National Australia Bank
    Sydney   (02) 237 1482
    Melbourne   (03) 573 3332
  Westpac   (02) 226 4916
Commonwealth   (02) 227 3532
(NB: Make sure they are not promoting particular franchises, otherwise their advice could be biased.)

Credit Reference Association of Australia (CRAA)

Victoria	(03) 670 7100
New South Wales	(02) 964 7555
Queensland	(07) 834 4700
Western Australia	(09) 480 3400
South Australia & Northern Territory	(08) 236 4222

General

Libraries, bookshops, weekly and daily magazines and newspapers, small business profiles.

233

Appendix

The following is an analysis of the connections between the three financial statements on pages 154–5:

Sales Revenue → Debtors

The balance in the Sales Revenue account is the sum of all sales made during the year. Assume that the company made all its sales on credit. The amount owed to the company is immediately recorded in Debtors when each sale is made. Later, when customers pay their debt, the cash account is increased and Debtors is decreased. The balance in Debtors is the amount of uncollected sales at the end of the year.

Of interest to the manager, creditors and investors alike is the average time taken to turn receivables into cash. The point is that the average sales credit period (ASCP) determines the size of debtors relative to annual sales revenue. The longer the ASCP the larger the debtors. Using information in financial statements we can determine the ASCP as follows:

$$52 \text{ weeks divided by } \frac{\$4{,}212{,}000 \text{ (sales revenue)}}{\$486{,}000 \text{ (debtors)}} = 6 \text{ weeks.}$$

Hence, at year-end, 6 weeks of the company's sales are still uncollected.

234

If the manager considers 6 weeks to be too long an ASCP, he or she can take certain steps to shorten it. If the company's ASCP had been only 5 weeks, the debtors would have been $81,000 less and the company would have collected $81,000 more in cash. At 10% interest on its borrowings the company would have saved $8100 before tax.

Cost of Goods Sold ←→ Inventory

The cost of goods sold is deducted from the sales revenue to determine the gross profit. Inventory is the amount of stock held at the end of the financial year and is shown in the balance sheet as an asset. Of interest to the manager, creditors and investors is how long the company holds an average item of stock before it is sold. The stock turnover ratio is most meaningful when it is used to determine the number of weeks it takes to sell stock. Using information in the financial statements we can determine the average inventory holding period (AIHP) as follows:

$$52 \text{ weeks divided by} \frac{\$2,808,000 \text{ (cost of goods sold)}}{\$702,000 \text{ (inventory)}} = 13 \text{ weeks.}$$

The AIHP determines the size of inventory relative to annual cost of goods sold. The longer the holding period, the larger the inventory. If the holding period is longer than necessary, too much capital is tied up in inventory or there is too much cash in inventory and not enough in the bank.

If the company could reduce its AIHP from 13 weeks to 11, $108,000 capital would be saved ($54,000 cost of goods sold per week × 2). However, the AIHP should not be so low that goods are not available as needed to make sales. The cost of carrying inventory has to be balanced against the profit opportunities lost by not having the products in stock.

Inventory → Creditors

When stock is purchased on credit the liability for the amount of goods bought is recorded in Creditors and the cost is recorded in Inventory.

235

Some purchases are paid for promptly while others are not paid for two months or so. Based on its payments experience and policies, a business can determine the average credit period it waits before paying for its stock purchases. In this example the average credit period is:

$$52 \text{ weeks divided by } \frac{\$2,808,000 \text{ (cost of goods sold)}}{\$216,000 \text{ (creditors)}} = 4 \text{ weeks.}$$

Sometimes the amount of creditors may be higher than normal where large purchases of stock are made just prior to year end or payment of bills is deliberately slowed down to conserve cash.

Operating Expenses → Creditors

Operating Expenses includes all expenses of running the business except for depreciation, which is shown separately. Some operating expenses are recorded before they are paid — for example, electricity or telephone bills received but not paid until the new financial year. Generally the credit terms of these Creditors are not long. In this example the average credit period of the company's unpaid operating expenses is:

$$52 \text{ weeks divided by } \frac{\$936,000 \text{ (operating expenses)}}{\$54,000 \text{ (creditors)}} = 3 \text{ weeks.}$$

Operating Expenses → Accrued Expenses (Payable)

Accrued Expenses would include such items as accumulated sick or annual leave pay, unpaid sales commission, part of annual rates and taxes or telephone costs that should be charged to this year but are not yet billed to the company. In this example the average credit period of the company's accrued expenses is:

$$52 \text{ weeks divided by } \frac{\$936,000 \text{ (operating expenses)}}{\$108,000 \text{ (accrued expenses)}} = 6 \text{ weeks.}$$

It will be seen that a total of 9 weeks' operating expenses are unpaid at year end (3 weeks' creditors and 6 weeks' accrued expenses). This relieved the company of a cash pay-out of $162,000 ($54,000 creditors plus $108,000 accrued expenses). If the company could have stretched the average credit period from 9 weeks to 11, it could have avoided an additional $36,000 of cash disbursements ($18,000 average weekly operating expenses × 2). In other words, creditors and accrued expenses resulting from operating expenses have a significant impact on cashflow.

Operating Expenses → Prepaid Expenses

Certain operating costs are paid in advance and not charged against revenue until later. They are initially recorded as prepaid expenses, which is an asset account, and each month a portion is transferred out of the Prepaid Expenses and recorded in expense.

In this example the company's prepaid expenses were equivalent to 5 weeks of its annual operating expenses:

$$52 \text{ weeks divided by } \frac{\$936,000 \text{ (operating expenses)}}{\$90,000 \text{ (prepaid expenses)}} = 5 \text{ weeks.}$$

If the manager could have reduced these prepayments from 5 weeks to 3, prepaid expenses would have been only $54,000, reducing the demand on cash by $36,000. On the other hand, if prepayments had been 7 weeks instead of 5, the cash demand would have been $36,000 more.

Property, Plant and Equipment → Depreciation → Accumulated Depreciation

The company owns desks, display cabinets, a computer system, various machines and tools, and so on, which are lumped together and recorded in one account called Machinery, Equipment, Furniture and Fixtures. These assets have a limited life span and are depreciated over each future year of expected use to the business.

237

In this example the company has assumed an average life of 4 years and depreciation is computed as follows:

$$\frac{\$464,000 \text{ machinery, equipment, furniture and fixtures}}{4 \text{ years useful life estimate}} = \$116,000 \text{ p.a.}$$

The amount of depreciation is not recorded as a decrease in the Assets account directly. Instead, it is added to the Accumulated Depreciation account and the balance of this account is deducted from the original cost of the assets.

It should be kept in mind that if the useful life estimate is too short, depreciation expense each year is too high.

Interest Expense → Accrued Expenses (Payable)

Interest is a financial cost as opposed to an operating cost. Interest is charged each day for the use of borrowed money and is usually paid quarterly or half-yearly. On both short- and long-term loans there is a delay in paying interest but the interest expense should be recorded for all days of the loan period. Any unpaid interest at the end of the accountancy period is recorded in Accrued Expenses, which is a liability account.

In this example, 9 weeks' interest is unpaid at year end:

$$52 \text{ weeks divided by } \frac{\$52,000 \text{ (interest expense)}}{\$9000 \text{ (accrued interest)}} = 9 \text{ weeks.}$$

Income Tax Expense → Income Tax Payable

A taxation liability is incurred by companies which earn profits, including capital gains. This is provided for in the balance sheet and expensed in the profit and loss statement in the year in which the profit is earned.

Net Income (Profit) → Retained Earnings

Net income is the final profit after deducting all expenses from the sales revenue. Retained earnings is the amount of net income earned and retained in the business. Dividends, if and when paid, are recorded as decreases in retained earnings.

In our example no dividends were paid to shareholders and the entire net income of $150,000 was retained in the business.

Retained Earnings keeps track of how much shareholders' equity was earned and retained in the business and is shown in the balance sheet separately from capital invested by shareholders (Paid-up Capital).

Bibliography

Byrt, W J & Pickett, Les 1971, *Personnel Management in Australian Industry and Commerce*, Institute of Personnel Management (Aust.)

Carew, Edna 1987, *The Language of Money*, George Allen & Unwin, London

Day, John K 1989, *Your Money and Your Life*, Lothian Publishing Company Pty Ltd, Melbourne

McCormach, Mark 1984, *What They Don't Teach You at Harvard Business School*, Collins, London

Mason, Jim 1990, *Advertising Without Tears — A Handbook for Small Business Professionals and Groups*, McCulloch Publishing Pty Ltd, Melbourne

Mogano, M 1980, *How to Start and Run Your Own Business*, Graham & Trotman Ltd, London

Ratnatunga, Janek & Dixon, John (eds) 1984, *Australian Small Business Manual*, CCH Australia

Samuelson, Paul A; Hancock, Keith; & Wallace, Robert 1970, *Economics — Australian Edition*, McGraw-Hill Book Company, Sydney

The Small Business Handbook 1990, Small Business Development Corporation, Schwartz & Wilkinson Publishers Pty Ltd, Division of Information Australia Group, Melbourne

Van Horne, James C 1971, *Fundamentals of Financial Management*, Prentice-Hall Inc., Englewood Cliffs, New Jersey

240

Index